Charlie

The Story of Charlie Gallagher, the GAA's Lost Icon

Paul Fitzpatrick

Ballpoint Press

Published in 2019 by Ballpoint Press
4 Wyndham Park, Bray,
Co Wicklow, Republic of Ireland.

Telephone: 00353 86 821 7631
Email: ballpointpress1@gmail.com
Web: www.ballpointpress.ie

ISBN 978-1-9998306-9-4

While every effort has been made to ensure the accuracy
of all information contained in this book, neither the author nor
the publisher accepts liability for any errors or omissions made.

Book design and production by Joe Coyle Media&Design,
joecoyledesign@gmail.com

Photographs: *The Anglo-Celt*, Tony Morris, James Brady,
Kevin Óg Carney, Tom Lynch, Frankie Kennedy and the
Gallagher family's personal collection.

Printed and bound by GraphyCems

Contents

This book is dedicated to my grandfather
Jimmy Brides (1938-2014).

Acknowledgements

When I began researching this book and speaking to people who knew Charlie Gallagher, the man and the footballer, something immediately jumped out. Charlie was not just an extraordinary individual — although he certainly was that – but he was also a man who was adored by all who knew him well and even those who did not.

That is a highly unusual thing, to be universally loved, to achieve so much in life and in sport and to make no enemies. It is almost unique. Then again, Charlie Gallagher *was* unique. He was a supremely-gifted sportsman, a brilliant dentist, a family man.

As a man, Charlie, they say, never really grew up. He retained his boyish, devil-may-care attitude to the end. And, on the pitch, he smashed records and he book-ended an era, in football and Irish life in general.

My late grandfather, to whom this book is dedicated, was born six months after Charlie and raised eight miles away from Cootehill and followed Cavan in the 1950s and '60s. The last match he attended was the 1969 Ulster final, Charlie's last. When Charlie retired from playing, Granda retired from supporting. It wasn't the same, he used to say.

Cavan football rose again only sporadically in the post-Gallagher years. The story of the sport became something of a sorrowful mystery but as I write, earlier this summer, Cavan qualified for the Ulster football final with swagger and style and the county was briefly capti-vated again. Who knows what the future holds.

Writing a book is a time-consuming job of work. To my wife Valerie, a heartfelt thanks for putting up with me and my late nights and distracted conversations.

The editor of this project was Paul Neilan, one of the sharpest literary minds I know. Thank you, Paul, for your guidance and knowledge.

A sincere thanks also to PJ Cunningham of Ballpoint Press for your encouragement and advice and to designer Joe Coyle, the best in the business.

To my father-in-law Donal Brady, a true and loyal Cavan supporter, a huge thanks for all your assistance from the throw-in to the final whistle.

The same goes for Larry McCluskey, Cootehill Celtic stalwart and an incalculable source of help with this proj-ect.

Thanks also to my editor at *The Anglo-Celt*, Linda O'Reilly, and Frank Mulrennan of Celtic Media Newspa-pers for their support always.

Most of all, I want to thank the Gallagher family for allowing and helping me to tell this story. Thank you to Maureen for such a warm welcome and to Adrian, Peter and Louise for sharing their memories of their father and helping in so many ways.

So many others helped me with this project. I wish to express my thanks to the following people for their assistance: Barney Cully, John Cully, Dessie Brady, Steve Duggan, Niall Brady, Finbar Brady, James Brady, Colm McAlarney, Savina Donohoe, Sean Boylan, Donie O'Sulli-van, Dessie O'Sullivan, Owen McConnon, Dermot Walsh, Michael McPhilips, Ian McCabe, Martin Brady, Gabriel Kelly, Ray Carolan, Paddy Maguire, MJ Clarke, Gene Cusack, Tom Lynch, Garrett O'Reilly, Msgr Ignatius McQuillan, Seamus Hoare, Sean Foy, Kevin Óg Carney, Joy Hayes, Paul Rouse, Tony Morris, Micheál Greenan, Donal O'Grady, Jim McDonnell, Phil 'Lightning' Murray, Kenny Connolly, Eamonn Gaffney, Seán Crosson, Shane Connaughton, Declan Coyle, Vincent Pilkington, Frankie Kennedy and Pat Nolan.

My favourite line in this book came from an old foe of Charlie's, who described him as "a bright light, a man who comes along once every 50 years."

Charlie has been gone for 30 years now but wherever football people gather to talk about the game, he will live on. I hope I have done his memory justice.

Paul Fitzpatrick
Virginia, Co Cavan
June, 2019

ONE

Wembley

It was May 15th, 1966, a sunny Sunday evening, and in Tommy Connolly's pub in Cootehill, the barber was bragging. Sean Foy, trainer of the local Celtics team, had arrived home early from a match in Carrickmacross, carrying with him word of a Cavan win that had secured the county team a trip to Wembley.

More importantly than that, a man born a couple of hundred yards away, down on Market Street, one Charlie Gallagher, had scored, Foy breathlessly informed the assembled drinkers, 1-10, a remarkable tally, against Ulster champions Down.

"I left the match a couple of minutes early and I was into the pub and I was blowing to the boys about the 1-10 Charlie scored," says Foy, still cutting hair, as he has done since opening his first shop in the town in 1947.

"And the next thing, this other fella came in and said Charlie got another goal after I left and it was 2-10 he got!"

The haul made headlines in all the papers but it was nothing new. Gallagher, 28, was the leading scorer in the country who, two years earlier, had been one of just seven GAA players selected to travel to the east coast of the United States for the prestigious John F Kennedy Memorial Games.

He was known in every town and village in the country. The assonance of his name. His magnetism. Charlie. Gallagher.

In a black and white era, he didn't just add a dash of colour — he illuminated the dowdy GAA scene. A dentist by profession, practising in Derry, Gallagher had it all — the looks, the skills, the swagger. Charlie had style and he had class. And, most of all, he was beloved.

In the 21st Century, he would have been a superstar. In the middle of the 20th, in conservative Ireland, dominated by Cootehill-born John Charles McQuaid's Church, he was a sensation.

The country had been decimated by emigration in the 1950s, rural areas hit hardest of all. The best and brightest had scattered to the four corners. By '66, little had changed. The unemployment rate was one of the highest in Europe and four times that of the UK.

"Nobody would have had very much back then," remembers James Brady, a teammate and at 83, still a practising vet. "Times were a lot tougher. It's like a thousand years ago, I can't describe how little a lot of people would have had growing up in the country in the 1950s."

But Gallagher, a graduate of UCD, dressed in sharp suits and drove a red Sunbeam Rapier sports car. A crowd would assemble in Cootehill of a Friday evening around the time he might be rolling into town, having come south from Derry for whatever match or training session was on.

He was single at the time, a man about town, cash on the hip. He was, many reckoned, the best forward in the sport. In the previous two seasons, '64 and '65, he had been the leading scorer in the country with tallies of 6-107 and 7-102, respectively — higher than totals being registered at the time by the leading hurlers.

An article in the match programme for the following year's Ulster final would reckon that, while earlier decades had not been rigorously collated, it was more than likely that Gallagher, not yet 30, was the highest scorer in the history of Gaelic football.

And when he would arrive home from Derry, he brought with him an entourage. A driver, maybe, or some supporters. People who were close, or wanted to be close.

"Everyone knew Charlie. He was a household name. And everyone that thought of Cavan thought of Charlie Gallagher," says Micheál Greenan, who would win two Ulster medals alongside him in later years.

"And as well as that, he was a shocking nice fella. He was never in a row, he would never insult anyone. He would just laugh, he was great fun. His life was just... take it easy and everything would fall into place."

Tom Lynch, who would win four Ulster senior medals alongside him in a golden decade, was aware of his team-mate's status.

"Charlie was probably the top sportsman in the country, or very close to it," says Lynch.

"Even though television coverage was very scant that time, he was recognised nationwide, way above most ordinary sportspeople.

"Charlie was unique. He had everything. He had the X factor, he was always well-dressed going out on the field, groomed immaculately. But we didn't look on him like that. He was a good team player and he just another teammate to us and very popular with everyone because he was so generous and full of good fun."

One-liners were Charlie's currency and trade was brisk. In team meetings, to the chagrin of legendary manager Mick Higgins, he would break the tension with a joke. He handled life on his own terms.

"He was a great character, great company," says Ray Carolan, another teammate with four Ulster medals.

"He lived in his own world a little bit. He loved the guys coming up talking to him, he'd thrive on it. And he'd say things that nobody else would get away with but he'd say it in such a funny and good-natured way.

"I remember being in the Antrim Arms in Drumcondra, which was owned by [Cavan All-Ireland winner] Joe Stafford, on a Sunday evening after a match in Croke Park and it came to nine o'clock and we were kind of saying 'we better hit the road, work tomorrow', or whatever.

"And Charlie says 'it's alright for you boys, if you miss a day, what are you losing, a tenner? If I miss a day's work, it will cost me a hundred pound!' He'd get away with that."

After the Cavan team had beaten All-Ireland three-in-a-row-seeking Down in a glorious Ulster final in Belfast in 1962, they went into camp at Kilnacrott, at a boarding school outside of Ballyjamesduff, which would in later years itself become notorious.

Most of the team took unpaid leave from their jobs to be there at a time when few would have had much to spare. Only a handful drove, others were still living at home.

Charlie, however, was a man of means, even though he placed little value on it.

"In the early sixties, we wouldn't have had much money," says teammate Gabriel Kelly.

"We'd come down in Joe Stafford's car from Dublin to train on Tuesdays and Thursdays. By Thursday night, you'd have frig all money because you'd be getting paid on a Friday.

"After training, we'd go down to the Farnham Hotel to get sandwiches. I remember Charlie would have arrived in his big car from Derry and he'd come and eat with us. I'd be saying, 'right lads, we'd better get back to Dublin, it'll be all hours' and Charlie would look at his watch and say 'ah, to hell with that. I'll stay here'. And he'd book himself into the Farnham for the night and pay for it. No problem to him at all."

In Kilnacrott, they had posed for a photograph, the whole group and, of course, one of the head priests. Gallagher sat dead centre, front row, in white trousers and shirt with a dark tie, grinning broadly. Higgins was on the end, wearing the priest's mitre.

It's hard, in fact, to find a team photo in which he is not front and centre, usually with a football at his feet. In another shot, Charlie has the mitre on. A crown for a prince.

"He used to attract people," recalls Garrett O'Reilly, a teammate in the Ulster successes of 1967 and 1969, whose father, TP, was county chairman and a hero of the All-Ireland wins of the 1940s.

"He wouldn't look for the quiet place. You'd go for a drink afterwards and fellas would be swarming round him. He was good fun to be with, he was good craic."

In Carrickmacross in '66, Down were heavily fancied. Their team was littered with All-Ireland winners and there was no question of fielding a weakened side. Not when there was a trip to London, to play in the final of the prestigious, fundraising Wembley tournament, at stake.

London, an hour's flight and a million miles from Small Town Ireland in the mid-'60s. London, where Muhammad Ali would fight Henry Cooper the following week and where Harold Wilson had just led Labour to a convincing win in a snap general election.

And Wembley. Two weeks earlier, the Beatles had played there. Two months after Cavan would take on Sligo, it would host the World Cup final. Wembley was a big deal then, a Promised Land.

It was a stage made for Charlie Gallagher.

Ten years earlier, to the week, it had held the FA Cup final, the only football match to be televised each season. That was the day Bert Trautmann, the Manchester City goalkeeper, broke his neck and played on. The 1956 final was also the last football match Fr Francis De Sales Gallagher ever saw. Charlie's brother, Frank, died a few days later, aged just 30.

So, Wembley resonated with Charlie. He had played there before in '63, losing to Kerry, and he wanted to get back.

Early in the qualifier in Carrickmacross, Gallagher sidled up to the legendary Down full-back Leo Murphy, 27 years old, holder of four Ulster and two All-Ireland medals and hard as a coffin nail.

Charlie saw his opening, knew that the Down men would have heard the reports of Cavan's poor form, of their loss to Armagh in the McKenna Cup a week earlier, of how even their own local press were writing them off.

"Go easy on me today, Leo," he said, cocking a thumb towards the sideline, "I'm not going well. I'm afraid they're going to drop me."

Gallagher's first chance was a free but he missed it by inches, striking the upright. Murphy may have been thinking that the line his man had spun him was true.

Down quickly opened an early three-point lead and

then Cavan got going, their powerful centre-back Carolan thundering through for 50-50 balls and, up front, Gallagher waltzing around tackles.

He grabbed two quick points and on 15 minutes, took a pass from John Nallen and found the net. Pat Tinnelly added another point and by half-time, it was Cavan 1-6 (Gallagher 1-5) to Down's 0-6.

In the second half, he added another five points before finishing with a second goal in the dying embers of the game, just as his clubmate, Foy, had left the ground. He had struck the woodwork twice, too.

"Gallagher was at least half a team in himself," recorded *The Irish Press*, "and both of his goals were brilliant efforts."

Two weeks later, Cavan were off to Wembley, flying from Aldergrove Airport in Belfast at 10 o'clock on a Friday night. The next day, they played Sligo in the Whit Weekend Wembley Tournament, the yearly fundraiser for the GAA in Britain, who would rent out 'the home of football'.

The team were billeted in Lancaster Gate, home of the English FA, and made their way to the stadium, which had been given a face-lift for the upcoming World Cup. Cavan won the toss and were allotted the home dressing-room.

"We walked into the dressing-room and there was a huge big bath, big enough to fit the whole team in," remembers wing-back Tony Morris, who made the first trip to Wembley in 1963.

"We weren't used to that kind of luxury, I can tell you."

Cavan had lost to Kerry in that maiden trip to London but three years later, they led most of the way, with goals from Phil 'Lightning' Murray and two from John

Joe O'Reilly, helping them to a comfortable 3-10 to 1-10 win before 30,000 fans, the number swollen by the coachloads who arrived from Birmingham, Liverpool, Coventry, Leeds and Manchester.

The trophy, three feet tall, had been donated by Tommy O'Gorman, a native of Lough Egish in Monaghan, who owned the famous Gresham Ballroom on the Holloway Road, at a cost of £300. The average weekly wage at the time was £20.

The only known surviving footage of Cavan in the 1960s was taken here and can be viewed on YouTube. The grainy, three-minute video — which features, if you look carefully, a celebrating streaker — shows Murray's brilliant goal and focuses on a beaming captain, Gallagher, accepting the cup in the royal box from the Irish Ambassador to Britain, John G Molloy. His Excellency later féted the team with a cocktail reception.

Thousands of Breffni exiles turned out for the match and over the weekend — the team would not return until Monday evening — their hotel, The Atlantic, was mobbed with Cavan people eager to meet their old friends.

Gallagher was the main attraction. Everywhere they went, people wanted to meet him and he had time for them all.

"He was great fun," says Steve Duggan, a 19-year-old sub on that trip who would grow into a key player and a great friend of Gallagher's.

"Everyone just wanted to be in his company. He was down to earth, just one of our own."

The next morning's *London People* would carry the match report, under the heading 'Charlie is Cavan's Darling'. And how he was.

(The reference was to 'Charlie Is My Darling', the title of an 18th Century traditional Scottish folk ballad and also the working title for a documentary on the Rolling Stones, which had been filmed earlier in '66 but was never released.)

On Saturday and Sunday night, the lads hit the town. Not that there was a big drinking culture — at least half were non-drinkers ("most fellas hadn't the money to drink," says one teammate) — but some liked a jar and a celebration after matches.

On Sunday morning, Higgins, the manager and holder of three All-Ireland medals himself, brought the whole group the couple of miles across town, through Hyde Park, to Stamford Bridge for greyhound racing. Higgins was a doggie man — in time, he would become a leading Irish trainer — and had a tip. A few of the team had a fiver on; the dog won.

A few photographs of Cavan's three 1960s trips to Wembley survive. One of the best is from '63, captured as a few players left Wembley in a taxi. In the back seat was Gallagher, his hands on the cup, alongside teammates Gabriel Kelly and Tony Morris.

"Smile, lads!" said someone from the front. And they obliged. Smiling came easily to Charlie — a wide, generous grin, jet black hair, eyes shining.

And when he smiled, they smiled. Because a wisecrack or a one-liner with Charlie Gallagher was the ordinary man's brush with the divine, the word made flesh.

"He was," says Duggan, "the Georgie Best of Gaelic football. People just loved him."

On the field, he was a marked man. Off it, like Best, he was, too.

TWO

Out Of The West

It began in the late 1700s; the great march of the linen workers. They came from Armagh and crossed the Shannon, heading west, thousands of refugees fleeing their homes.

While they trekked, Armagh burned. Penal laws, which had kept the Catholic underclass down, had been slowly relaxed and some of the Protestants wished to re-assert their supremacy.

Catholics were starting to enter the lucrative, Protestant-dominated linen market and beginning to come into some money, but their bids on property were raising the price of land.

Industrialisation was increasing and wages, for the ruling class, had plummeted. Protestants felt under siege again. The pot came to the boil. All hell broke loose.

The Peep O'Day Boys — so-called because of their habit of raiding Catholic homes at day-break — were on the prowl. Catholics responded by forming the Defenders.

Tit-for-tat violence and retaliation ensued. In January 1791 in Forkhill, where Catholics were a majority, a mob attacked a local Protestant schoolteacher and his wife and son, cutting off their tongues.

The following July, after a tub-thumping address at a Battle of the Boyne commemoration in Drumcree, a gang of Protestants toured the district brutalising their enemies. Such mobs were known as 'the wreckers' and their activities have been described as ethnic cleansing.

"This unprovoked atrocity of the Protestants revived and redoubled religious rancour," noted an account in 1809. "The flame spread and threatened a contest of extermination..."

In September, 30 Defenders were killed near Loughgall, after which a group retired to a local pub and formed the Orange Order. There was now no going back.

Cootehill, in Co Cavan, was the linen capital of Ireland and a "hotspot of discontent", too. When the United Irishmen were formed four years earlier, bringing Catholics and Presbyterians together, they had begun to heavily recruit there and by '98, they would battle the Crown forces at Rebel Hill outside Bailieborough, in a vain attempt to prevent reinforcements from making it to Castlebar.

Just down the road from Castlebar was Louisburgh, a planned town on the Bunowen River, which had been founded in 1795 to accommodate some of the thousands of fleeing Catholics, driven west in the purges.

Soon, the area grew. By 1841, Mayo had a population of 388,000 but the county, where 90 per cent of the population was dependent on the potato, was ravaged by the Great Famine.

In 1849, an estimated 600 of the poorest residents — those who had less than a quarter of an acre to their names — set out to walk 12 miles around Doolough ('the Black Lake') for Delphi Lodge, where they were to be inspected by two government agents, Colonel Hogrove and Captain Primrose, who were to distribute 3lbs of grain to each if they warranted it.

They walked through the night, through rain, wind and

sleet, "unfortunate half-skeletons", and local lore says that those who made it alive were made to wait until the gentlemen had had their lunch. And then they were sent on their way, empty-handed. Some estimates reckon that 400 perished, some blown into the lake because they were too weak to stand up, others strewn along the roadside.

That was the landscape in Louisburgh into which, a generation later, Thomas 'Bernie' Gallagher was born in Bridge Street, the eldest son of Patrick Gallagher from Aitnaveen and his wife, Kate Coyne, Ballyhip.

Patrick and Kate leased a pub, The Trading Post — which is now a craft shop — and Bernie was sent to boarding school in St Jarlath's, 50 miles away in Tuam.

As the eldest boy, he was being groomed for the priesthood and in time, he did take that route. But after six weeks in Holy Cross College, a seminary in Drumcondra, he decided the priesthood wasn't for him and returned home.

What happened next is shrouded in some mystery but the story — a whisper — handed down in the family was that Kate wasn't happy that she hadn't raised a man of the cloth. Outraged, she banished her boy from the home and he moved across the road and in with his aunt, Annie Scahill.

Annie had returned from the States a widow with two young boys and, in time, she would pay for her nephew to go to medical college in Galway, from where he graduated in 1923. Mrs Scahill's two sons, as it happens, became priests themselves.

Bernie was headstrong, as bad as his mother. He made a different vow, they say, there and then: never to return home to Louisburgh on account of Kate's actions. Years later, he would turn the car for the West and the closer to home he got, his family noticed, the cheerier he became and the louder he sang. But there was a line on the map he would not cross; the doctor would stop short of Louisburgh, not even returning to see his aunt.

But that was all well in the future. Upon graduation, Bernie moved to England and, two years later, the year he married Eva Corrigan from Castleblayney, Co Monaghan, he returned and set up practice 10 miles south of her hometown in Carrickmacross. He was a learned man, well-read in his field, taking a diploma in midwifery in Holles Street in 1928 and a further degree the following year.

But the sky darkened. The doctor, soon a father of seven, liked a drink. After an abdominal illness in 1932, he became prone to depression, "bad with his nerves". And in 1934, he was involved in a tragic incident which was likely the second dramatic, defining event of his life.

On June 20th, he was in Dublin to attend the Central Criminal Court as a witness in a case of infanticide. The case, he would later say in court, had caused him "untold anxiety".

He sank a bottle of bromide mixture and some luminal tablets in the hope that he would sleep. The next morning, he met a friend, a Mr Ward, whose mother he had lodged with in his student days. The men had a drink, a few bottles of stout, he would claim, in town, then drove out to Lucan, where they had another couple and then a couple more in Knightsbridge.

As he returned up Benburb Street, a Mary Tracey was out walking her four-month-old baby in a pram alongside her husband, Tom, a 22-year-old soldier at McKee Barracks. At the corner of Queen Street and the Bridewell Lane, Gallagher came down the wrong side of the street, swerved and struck them.

Tom died the next morning. When Gallagher was examined in the Garda station, he was found to be drunk, his speech slurred, unable to properly pronounce the word 'Rockcorry', the town where he had recently been appointed doctor.

The trial, a few months later, made national news. A character witness, a priest, testified that he considered the doctor "a teetotaller". But Gallagher was found guilty of manslaughter — the jury were split and urged clemency — and was handed a six-month sentence.

In January, he was removed from office in Rockcorry, against the wishes of the local community. Soon, though, he had set up a practice on Market Street in Cootehill, five miles away across the county boundary in Cavan, that centre for the linen trade we mentioned before.

It was a new start. And on Christmas Day 1937, came a gift; an eighth child for Bernie and Eva, who already had Frank, Leonora, Eva, Una, Brian, Angela and Nuala. It was a third son. They named him Charles.

THREE

The Rising

In June, 1956, St Patrick's College opened a brand new football pitch and produced an impressive commemorative booklet to mark the occasion. Fr Patrick Gargan, who had been training the school teams since 1942, penned an article recounting the history of football in the school.

"I have been often asked is it difficult to train a college team," he wrote.

"The answer is no. No concessions, no special diet or extra time for recreation are required."

St Pat's, with one small pitch on the side of a hill, had made the breakthrough at MacRory Cup level in 1935 and, in the 20 years that followed, reached another nine finals, winning seven to establish themselves as the leading football school in the province.

Football meant everything in the college, which in 1950, the year Charlie Gallagher enrolled, had 66 boys to call on. The net result was that by the dawn of the 1940s, Cavan senior teams were dominated by graduates of St Pat's, most by then drawn from the professional classes.

On the Cavan side which won the All-Ireland in the Polo Grounds in 1947, for example, there were a couple of vets, a solicitor and future judge, a schoolteacher and future Tánaiste, a handful of Gardaí, a commandant and a lieutenant in the Irish army, almost all of them St Pat's old boys.

James McCabe, an international banker, and Tom Hardy, a doctor, had won MacRory medals in 1948 and went on to win All-Ireland medals with Cavan in 1952, as did Brian Gallagher, then a medical student, who had picked up his MacRory medal in '51.

"There were never that many farmers on the Cavan team. Maybe away back in the '30s but not in my time," says Jim McDonnell, who played on the side beaten in the 1952 MacRory Cup final and would return to spend 40 years on the teaching staff.

"They had too much work to do, I suppose, they hadn't much time to train. Fellas in college got a better chance, I think anyway. At home, fellas would maybe have to milk the cows when they got home, it wouldn't be out to the football field they go."

The profile of the Cavan teams of those eras was not unusual, says historian Paul Rouse.

"There is this fascinating story about class and the GAA. There is this illusion that it was for 'all movements' but the reality is that the GAA was for all classes but that it was actually based on professionals.

"If you go through the whole thing, there is a bit of a myth there about the GAA. It wasn't a new thing for a professional to be a footballer in the 1940s or 1950s. There's a general growth in the country of better educated people getting better jobs but even before that there's the Fitzgibbon and Sigerson cups and what they did with that.

"There's always been this idea of the GAA as being 'racy of the soil' but it's too simplistic. There was also that pride in education and education being the break in the poverty of families. People won a lot of scholarships and then farmers might send their kids to college, to try to push them on a bit."

That was the case in most of the long-established Catholic-run secondary schools, which, while experiencing a surge in enrolments, were still conservative and almost Victorian in outlook.

St Patrick's College in Cavan was a dark place. The clerics ruled with an iron fist and the food — what there was of it — was appalling.

"I had a sister who was a nurse in the surgical in Cavan got a half day on a Wednesday and she used to come out and give me a bit of food. You'd be starving," recalls James Brady, who entered in 1949 and ended up qualifying as a vet, achieving first place in the country in his final exams.

Football was the main outlet of expression. If you could play ball, you had a chance.

That would not change for the longest time. Twenty years later, Paddy McGill, who arrived from England into an alien world and adapted to star on the Hogan Cup-winning team of 1972, would describe the culture in the school as "kill or be killed".

"My first two years in St Pat's were savage. Imagine being a Coventry kid sent over to St Pat's in 1966. I played my first game of football when I was 14 years of age, I didn't know what Gaelic football was. But there was nothing else to do in St Pat's. If you played, you had some status. I loved it then."

Frankie Kennedy, future Cavan defender, also attended the school, a couple of years behind Gallagher, and would play in two MacRory finals himself.

"It was a tough place. If you played football, it wasn't as bad but the priests always kept you down. You weren't allowed to read the newspapers. I was selected as Ulster Colleges Footballer of the Year in 1958, it was chosen by the GAA writers.

"But I was never told about it in St Pat's — I learned about that five years later when a guy sent me a cutting from the paper. That's the way it was, the priests kept you down."

Gallagher's brothers' reputations — Brian was part of Cavan's 1952 All-Ireland-winning senior squad and Frank had been a classy player too — would have ear-marked him as a kid with potential but it was soon clear that he was special.

"He was always brilliant, he could do anything with a ball from he was 12, 13 years of age," says Dessie O'Sullivan, a neighbour and contemporary of Gallagher's. "It was always there."

The MacRory Cup was an under-18 competition. At 15, in October 1953, Gallagher broke into the team, lining out in a 10-3 to 1-7 win over St Eunan's, Letterkenny, who featured in goals Seamus Hoare, alongside whom he would later win five Railway Cup medals.

A win over St Macartan's before Christmas set up a final tilt against Newry CBS on March 7th. The Cavan boys were fancied to win and got the train to Armagh for the final, buzzing with expectation.

Now, Charlie wasn't the only Gallagher on the pitch. The referee was 39-year-old Patrick 'PJ' Gallagher from Omagh, an optician and father-of-one who had played senior inter-county football for Tyrone. Both of his brothers were priests.

On a heavy surface which was compared to "a ploughed field", a point from Gallagher just before half-time saw St Pat's lead by 1-2 to 0-3.

At midfield, James Brady and Tom McCabe were dominating and Cavan were in control.

"The team were playing really well," recalled Brady. "We were going to win it, I have no doubt."

But moments into the second half, there was a commotion and when the players turned around, the referee was on the ground. He was immediately removed to the side of the pitch, where he died within minutes.

"We were waiting for a kick-out and I was only a couple of feet away from him. The referee dropped dead."

The replay was six weeks later in Ballybay and Newry won it.

The following year, though, Charlie would get his hands on that MacRory title, the first major success of his career. St Pat's defeated St Malachy's from Belfast in the decider, 2-8 to 0-2, in Armagh.

A week later, Gallagher was chosen at left-half forward — his usual spot in those days — for the second year in succession, on the Ulster Colleges side to play Connacht in Sligo in the All-Ireland interprovincial series. His star was rising.

¶ ¶ ¶ ¶

By the summer of 1955, three years had passed since Cavan had been All-Ireland champions and hopes were high in the county that they could go all the way again. The senior team duly beat Monaghan, Tyrone and Armagh to win the Ulster title and set up an All-Ireland semi-final against Kerry.

It was then that the calls began to be heard to bring Charlie Gallagher, still a schoolboy, straight into the

senior side. Gallagher's underage and colleges perfor-
mances had the county humming with chatter and even
though the seniors had been scoring heavily in the provincial championship, the calls still rang out to select the
Cootehill youngster, still just 17-and-a-half years of age,
for the All-Ireland semi-final.

"Many Cavan followers were anxious to see a place
allotted in the forward line to Charlie Gallagher, brother of Brian's," noted *The Anglo-Celt*, "following his many
excellent displays in club and minor county games."

A late December birthday is always a hindrance in
underage Gaelic games, where the cut-off date for eligi-
bility is January 1st, but it didn't affect Gallagher. In June
of 1954, aged 16, he made his county minor debut, scoring
0-3 in a big win over Fermanagh on the undercard to the
seniors' win over Monaghan in which Brian landed 0-5.
Both Gallaghers wore the number 10 jersey.

But while the seniors asserted control of what was
their own personal fiefdom by winning the Ulster title
again — they had been shocked by Armagh in 1953, a por-
tent of things to come later in the decade — the minors
were knocked out by Down in the semi-final.

The following year, the *Celt* lauded Charlie's "brilliant
play" in a narrow win over Monaghan at Kingscourt in
the opening round of the Ulster Minor Championship
but, although they were "wildly fancied" to beat Antrim
in the final, Cavan collapsed.

In the match report, where the rest of the team made
do with initials and surnames, Charlie was the only player whose full first name was listed; already he was being
marked out as something different, something distinct.

"Cavan's outstanding player was Charlie Gallagher, who did all that one man could do to turn the game around," noted the match report.

It was no surprise, then, that there were calls for him to be included on the senior team for the Kerry game.

"Charlie was tailor-made to be a star. He had a very presentable image, was a good-looking fellow, and possessed a sort of charisma that is not found nowadays among even the most talented of players," Cavan senior player of the 1950s, Jimmy 'Inky' Sheridan, would recall.

"He was famous even at minor age, more famous even at minor level than many a senior inter-county player."

And it was no wonder — before he was officially an adult, he had two Senior Championship medals to his name.

¶ ¶ ¶ ¶

There has always been something of a swagger about Cootehill Celtic. They are what is known in the Gaelic games idiom as 'a townie team'. And, in the parlance, that means skill and flair, a measure of class.

Rural clubs traditionally viewed those from urban areas as having a soft underbelly. In the country areas, farming was the dominant occupation and the characteristics inherent in that job — courage, durability, physical strength — mirrored those prized in football defenders.

So it was that the saying used to go that in rural counties like Cavan and Kerry, the country teams provided the backs, the townies produced the forwards. Like all clichés, there was a measure of truth in there somewhere.

The Cootehill club was formed in 1894 at a time when

emigration was rife in Cavan, the population of which dropped by 12.85pc between 1891 and 1901.

Cootehill was "quite a Protestant town" at the time and devotees of that faith had largely turned their back on the fledgling Gaelic Athletic Association, which, while espousing non-sectarian ideals, was fiercely nationalist in outlook. That may explain why it took so long, relatively speaking, for a GAA club to be formed.

According to Hugh O'Brien's excellent official history of the club, a man called McCudden, from a clan of cattle and pig dealers in the town, had left for Glasgow, as did Tommy McBreen, a tailor and another individual with two of the finest nicknames one will hear, Tom 'The Duster' 'Bird-in-the-Hand' Kelly.

All were fans of Glasgow Celtic as was Micky Lynch, who also had a grá for Belfast Celtic having been reared in that city. After a time, the lads got together and decided to set up a soccer club in Cootehill.

Others, though, wanted to establish a Gaelic club and somewhere along the way, the soccer element got dropped. The homage to both Celtics remained, though, in the name and the famous green and white hoops.

It took 31 years before the club made their first final, losing to Gowna. In 1932, from nowhere, they beat the famed Cornafean to win the Senior League title, with the USA Silver Cup — in the shape of a football — displayed in the window of Jack Smith's chemist shop in Market Street, not far from what would soon be the Gallagher family home, for the following 12 months.

Man of the Match was Hughie O'Reilly, who would go on to star at midfield in Cavan's All-Ireland successes in 1933 and '35 and train the All-Ireland-winning sides of

1947, '48 and '52. The other Cootehill stars of the era were Cavan's Louis Blessing and Willie Connolly, the latter of whom died from tuberculosis aged 27 in 1938.

By 1947, Cootehill were languishing in junior ranks, where they were making little impact. Some of the younger players decided that they should apply to be regraded to senior anyway in order to increase motivation. Things picked up for a while but by 1950, they were in the basement again.

The following year, the revival began. Brian Gallagher scored 2-5 in the quarter-final win over Kingscourt and they beat Ballyconnell in the semi to reach a rare county championship final against Castlerahan.

By the time the big day came around in Virginia, numbers were low — two clerical students cried off and the full-back was injured. Hughie O'Reilly, aged 47, was called back into action. Castlerahan won.

"Hughie playing was the downfall," says Foy.

"There was a young fella, Joe McGrath, he came off the field crying and I went over to him and said, 'what are you crying for?' and he said, 'Hughie Reilly shouldn't have been on that team'."

But Hughie would play a key role in the following seasons as team trainer. In 1952, a meeting was held in Connolly Brothers on Bridge Street and the players made a pact to train harder than ever, pledging to rise early in the morning and take to the pitch for an hour before heading to their day's work.

It paid off. In October, Brian Gallagher won an All-Ireland medal with Cavan as they saw off Meath in a replay. And on December 21st, Brian and his young Cootehill teammates finally won the club's first Junior Championship by beating Butlersbridge.

Further glory followed. In the first year of their return to senior level, the Celtics went all the way to the final, where they were pitted against the might of Cornafean. The Reds, who had 19 Senior Championships to their name, were overwhelming favourites, but an early penalty from Brian Gallagher set the underdogs on their way and they caused a sensation with a 3-5 to 0-3 success.

The townies had beaten the country men and had done so in style. The record attendance of 3,000 — the majority said to be from Cootehill — was proof that Hughie's young team had captured the imagination. Bonfires licked the sky and illuminated the shopfronts on their return.

Little did anyone know — or maybe they did — that the best of them all was watching on and waiting for his chance.

¶ ¶ ¶ ¶

Towards the end of 1953, 15-year-old Charlie Gallagher had been thrown in for his debut for the Cootehill senior team in a tournament game against Meath club Syddan in Kingscourt.

By the following June, he had nailed down a starting place, making his Senior Championship debut in the opening round as Cootehill confirmed their superiority over the Reds. They went on to reach the final against another of the rural giants, Mullahoran, whom they brushed aside easily. In the team photograph, Charlie stands on the extreme left, impossibly young-looking. Yet he played his part and was fast becoming a key figure in the best side the club would produce and, overall, one of the greatest in the 130-year history of the competition.

In 1955, that Cootehill team, powered on by the Gallagher brothers' scoring ability, peaked. They cruised to a third Senior Championship, this time beating Kingscourt in the final, and, in October, went about adding the league title.

When they saw off Cornafean in the semi-final, *The Anglo-Celt* described Charlie as "by far the best player on the field". Next time out, Mullahoran were again the victims. Cootehill Celtic, it seemed, were unstoppable.

Just as in boxing, the blows which sting most are the ones you don't see coming. On July 1st the following year, Cootehill lined out against Kingscourt in the first defence of their title, having not lost a championship match in almost five years.

Having dominated the Stars so many times in the intervening period, a measure of complacency maybe had set in. Brian Gallagher was absent, away in Spain on a trip which his late brother Fr Frank, six weeks dead, had booked. There were injuries, too, and a last-minute goal sank the Celtics.

Cornafean stole in and won their 20th Senior Championship. To date, neither of those famous clubs has added another.

FOUR

UCD

If you know of Brian Gallagher, you know this: he was the doctor who refused to charge a fee. Mention his name to anyone — anyone — who knew him and that will be the first sound to echo back. The second will usually be the fact that he was Charlie's brother; his All-Ireland medal a distant third.

Brian qualified from UCD in 1957 and, two years later, married Grace O'Connor from Limerick and established himself at a practice in Middlesex in England.

He would return to Cootehill for football matches and eventually to work, where he became a much-loved local figure. They called him 'the half-a-crown doctor' — he would ask for a pittance, often nothing at all. It was a trait Charlie shared in later years, when they both worked in their hometown. They valued kindness and decency more than cash.

Brian's obituary, after his passing in 2008, spoke of how he was "never interested in money".

"In his consciousness and in his view of the world there were more important things in life than financial wealth — he saw himself as another mere mortal treading the journey of life and whatever help he could give to others in making that journey he would do so."

Brian was a non-drinker and, in actual fact, detested alcohol. He lived for his work, his family and football.

Physically, he resembled Charlie although Brian was taller and thinner, taking after his father, whose practice he would take over in 1968.

For a couple of years, Brian and Charlie were together in Dublin, staying in digs a mile from UCD with a family named Roberts. They kept themselves to themselves at that stage. Brian, four years the elder sibling, was in charge.

At weekends, they gathered up the other locals in the capital and came home for club and county matches.

"They would come down from Dublin; five or six of them in a car. Money was very scarce at that time and the Gallaghers never charged for the car," remembers Sean Foy, who was club treasurer around then.

"They brought whoever was in Dublin and they paid for the car hire. That was a big thing that time. They looked after that."

For some reason — maybe because he wasn't keen on the socialising that went with it, although he had a warm personality, too — Brian did not tog out for the UCD Sigerson Cup team in his time at the college, which was highly unusual for a player of his stature; an All-Ireland medalist and free-taker on the Cavan side.

Charlie, though, did, from his second year onwards. The Sigerson was made up of four teams at the time, UCD, UCG, UCC and Queen's University. The format was as follows: both semi-finals were played on a Saturday and the final the following afternoon, with the venue for the annual competition rotating around the four colleges each year.

Cavan were strongly represented in UCD, with Jim McDonnell, James Brady, Brian O'Reilly and Cathal

Young lining out on the Sigerson-winning team of 1957. Into the mix for the following year came Charlie and he quickly settled into the side.

His first Sigerson Cup weekend was in December, 1958. James McCabe, a brother of Tom's from Gallagher's Mac-Rory team — Jim later became Chief Education Officer at the World Bank in Paris — had recently graduated but was still friendly with his former Cavan teammates.

Sigerson weekend was in Galway. McCabe had a car and offered to do the driving and Gallagher, McDonnell and Brady jumped aboard, eschewing the train for McCabe's black VW Beetle.

"James had played with UCD but he was working by this stage — he was one of our own. He was a Cavanman and he was just going to watch, he was part of the scene and he said, 'look, I'll bring you down'," recalls Brady.

"So, we headed down from Dublin, McDonnell and Gallagher and James McCabe and myself and sure, we were all delighted to be travelling down together for the weekend."

Traditionally, Queen's were the weakest of the four and had never won the competition. The way it usually worked — an unspoken rule — was that the host college would rig the draw and take on the Belfast side in the semi, letting the other two go to war before picking over the bones the next day. And when it would come to the final, the home team would have the advantage.

On this occasion, though, Queen's caused a sensation by beating UCG, and with UCD beating Cork, a novel final was in store in Fahy's Field in Salthill.

With 20 minutes to go, UCD were winning easily when their star midfielder Frank O'Leary was brutally taken out of the game and Queen's rallied to force a draw. And that's when the craic really started.

"Always on the Sunday night there would be a dinner and a dance after the final, the home team put that up for the other teams," says Brady.

"So, we were all at this and we had to get back home to Dublin that night because I had an exam in the veterinary college at nine o'clock the next morning.

"Anyway, all the boys were there at the dance and Jesus, for the first time ever, didn't I see Gallagher with a glass of beer in his hand. And him drinking it. That was the first night he ever drank and he was as drunk as a lord. And so was McDonnell. And so was McCabe!

"Now this was one o'clock of a winter's night in some dance hall in Galway and — I never drank to this day — I was left with three drunken men and a Volkswagen car... and I had never driven it! I had barely ever driven any car before and I had to be in Dublin the next morning at nine o'clock for an exam!

"The dance finished and we had to go and McCabe says to me, 'Jesus, James, you'll have to drive!' After a struggle, I eventually got McDonnell and Gallagher into the back seat of the Beetle and McCabe sat in the passenger seat.

"And as true as I'm sitting here, there was a fog and you wouldn't see the front of the car. That time you wouldn't be travelling around the country and I didn't have a bull's notion how I'd get to Dublin from the heart of Galway at that hour of the night.

"I came duking along anyway out of the city and came on out about a half a mile and I saw what looked like a signpost; black and white stripes. I was within about five feet of it... So, I got out of the car and cracked a match and looked up at the signpost and on it, it said 'Dublin'. 'Oh, Jesus,' I said, 'I'm right!'

"I got into the car and it was surely two o'clock by that time and I arrived back in Dublin at seven o'clock in the morning. And the boys fast asleep in the car.

"I dropped them off at their digs, left the car for McCabe to lift later, handed him the keys, got a bus and headed to Ballsbridge to sit my exam."

Six weeks later, Charlie would celebrate his 21st birthday.

¶ ¶ ¶ ¶

The replay took place the following February in Ballybay and, against all the odds, Queen's won the cup for the first time.

UCD's attention turned to the Dublin Senior Football Championship, of which St Vincent's were the undisputed kings. They hadn't lost a match — any kind of match — in Dublin between 1949 and 1956 until UCD, pre-Gallagher, beat them in a league game. Later that year, 'the Vinnies' would lose the county final to Erin's Hope but they would bounce back to win six more in succession.

The GAA's rules had changed in 1955 to allow players line out for both their college team and their home clubs in county championships, which immediately created resentment. The students were seen as interlopers from the country and the rivalry between them and St Vincent's, led by Kevin Heffernan, was vicious and would grow much worse throughout the 1960s and '70s, particularly after UCD would end their run in '63.

In June, 1959, UCD — who had won the Senior League final before Christmas — defeated Parnell's by five points to reach their first county final since the new rules had been brought in, with Gallagher landing 0-9.

In the final, it was St Vincent's again. The champions scored three goals in the opening three minutes with two from 'Heffo', but 0-8 from Gallagher helped the students overhaul them before a final twist.

Cathal Young, who attended the game as a supporter, would recall the "devastating" feeling when Paddy Farnan won it late on for St Vincent's on a freakish scoreline of 5-3 to 2-10.

So, it was back to the Sigerson for Gallagher and his buddies, this time in Cork.

The country was flooded that December weekend, with torrential rain sweeping Munster in particular. UCD qualified for the final with a bit to spare thanks to two goals from Brady and took on the hosts in what were, according to one report, "truly wretched conditions".

"It was like a place at the back of a gate where you'd have 100 cows standing. And it was a ferocious wet day, a desperate day and the pitch was unbearable," remembers Brady.

UCC were out to stop the Dublin college from spoiling their party. Gallagher was targeted; in truth, any player with skill was in that competition.

The Sigerson was infamous for its physicality. Padraic Gearty, UCD goalkeeper on the 1955 team, observed that: "Sigerson games were extremely tough, referees tended to let a lot go".

Up until the 1960s, in fact, no player was ever sent off in a Sigerson match. "Don't be afraid," the referee, a Kerryman, told Brady before the 1959 semi-final, "to hit these fuckers. I won't put you off."

"It seemed as if players could get away with anything in the Sigerson," said Cathal Young.

(As an aside; Benny Gaughran, writing in UCD football club's short-lived magazine, *Tidings*, would describe an incident in the 1964 final against Queen's. UCD's Paddy O'Hanlon — a future MP and a founder member of the SDLP — was flattened by "a perfectly-timed shoulder charge which had the effect of stunning him momentarily. The defender lay prone on the Casement Park sod, inert, the ball still tightly in his grasp". Gaughran went on to note that the referee was "within his rights in awarding a 14-yard free against the unconscious defender".)

But while UCC were lining Gallagher up, his uncanny ability to ride challenges, often airborne as he shipped hits, shone. And on this dog of a day came a goal regarded as one of the greatest in the history of the competition.

"As in their semi-final victory over Queen's on Saturday, UCD were first to score and it was a Cavanman again who put them on the road to victory," reported *The Irish Independent*.

"But whereas James Brady had the honour on the previous day, it was Charlie Gallagher here who made a jinking run at high speed to send a bullet-like drive to the net in the 11th minute."

Brady can still remember it clearly.

"In the first few minutes, Gallagher got this ball about 50 yards out and he dummied and twisted and turned around about four fellas and from about 20 yards out he left fly and buried a mighty goal. And we went on and beat them well."

UCD ran out 3-8 to 1-4 winners and Gallagher had a Sigerson medal to add to his Cavan Senior Championship and MacRory Cup ones.

The party started immediately. The banquets were legendary.

"I remember going to one Sigerson dinner out in Killiney after I had finished in UCD," said Young.

"There was a good spirit from the start. 'Molly Malone' got a rattle from the Dublin hosts, then 'Galway Bay' was sung by UCG followed by 'The Banks of My Own Lovely Lee' by the Corkmen. Finally, the Queen's lads started singing 'The Men Behind The Wire' and all joined in. This was before the meal had even begun..."

There was a denouement to the tale. A week later, *The Sunday Independent*'s Gaelic games columnist Andy Croke hit out at the culture of violence in Sigerson matches.

"I know football is not for weaklings and I know the Sigerson Cup has a reputation for toughness," he wrote.

"But I draw the line when a player goes into a tackle with both knees up and his elbow extended in the general direction of his opponent's jaw... I draw the line when a player, after getting rid of the ball, is practically buried in the mud."

Supporters in that era often viewed silken ball-players with a degree of suspicion and it was an accusation that would sometimes be levelled at Gallagher during his career — he wasn't, some would say, tough enough. But he had proven in the harshest theatre of all that he had the will to go with the skill.

Not that Charlie ever hit back.

"The tackling that time was very heavy. There would be a fella with his arms around Charlie's neck and another fella punching the ribs of him," remembers Foy of club and county matches.

"It was the only way they could stop him."

Foy recalls a Cootehill versus Bailieborough Shamrocks match in which the Shamrocks' full-back held Gallagher by the jersey for the entire match and did not let go.

"At half-time, I went over to Charlie, there was an ould dressing-room in Cavan that time, and I said, 'will you hit that fella a f**kin' thump'!"

Gallagher wouldn't hear of it.

"'I came here to play football,' he says. I never forgot that. He made me feel small," says Foy.

A supporter got vengeance for him, in any case, even if Gallagher didn't want it. The referee, who had allowed the fouling to go on, was Cavan All-Ireland winner Simon Deignan. When the final whistle blew, an incensed Cootehill fan invaded the pitch and dropped the referee, whistle and all.

FIVE

The Making
Of A Marksman

Practice. Always practice. For place-kickers, there is no other way.

Charlie was never the hardest trainer; he didn't relish the long runs and the slog. His game wasn't based on that anyway. In Gaelic football, the true marksmen want numbers after their name; get the ball, shoot. Rinse and repeat.

Wherever he was, when he would go to practise frees, he would bring some helpers, youngsters who might be knocking around. When the session was over, he would throw them a jersey or a few shillings — a bumper haul for any wide-eyed kid.

"When Cavan won Ulster in 1969, I was seven and I was old enough at that stage to go out to the meadow," recalls Kevin Óg Carney, who grew up a few doors away from the Gallaghers.

"That was Moorehead's meadow, where Celtic Park was, opposite the Errigal Hotel. We would go out on our bikes and kick the ball back to him when he would be practising frees.

"Not far from the goals was a river and you had to be careful not to let the ball go into the river and I remember that Charlie would pop them just over the bar. Quite a few would even ricochet off the bar. He was gliding them over and that was such a skilful art in itself; he was doing it so the ball wouldn't go into the river because he didn't want us, as children, going near it to retrieve the ball.

"He was very generous, he always had bags of sweets for us, which made it even better because, at that stage, we knew how big of an icon he was."

In open play, Gallagher was about speed and a poacher's instinct, administering his assassin's temperament the instant after gathering close to goal. They said he didn't like to pass; he would good-naturedly joke that he had nobody to pass to.

"People used to say Charlie was selfish," says Steve Duggan, "but I can tell you this because I played with him: Charlie was never selfish. If Charlie was going in on a solo run, I might have been beside him and we'd be all shouting for the ball. 'Charlie! Charlie!'

"But Charlie could put the ball over the black spot himself from 50 yards with right or left foot. He was that good. Why should he pass it to me for the sake of it when he could do that?

"It wasn't that he was selfish, it was just that he knew that he had that ability. No way was Charlie selfish."

Phil 'Lightning' Murray, like many of Gallagher's former teammates, agrees.

"Was he selfish? No. We would give him the ball. He was always available and you knew that if you gave him the ball at the right time, he was probably going to score."

Physically, he was well built — "he was deceptively strong in the upper body," says Tom Lynch — but not barrel-chested. He had a low centre of gravity and amazing balance.

"A thing I did notice about Charlie, funny as it sounds, was that he had small feet," says Micheál Greenan. "I suppose his margin for error was smaller when striking the ball."

Not tall, like his father and his brother, but not small. Compact, you could say, with a dancer's grace.

"One of the things made him dangerous was that he had blistering pace over about five yards. And it's the first five yards that usually counts," says Seamus Hoare.

Duggan was 19 when he broke through to the team in '67 as an earth-scorching wing-forward. Gallagher was 30, yet Duggan couldn't catch him.

"We'd be doing ten-yard sprints in Virginia and, even though I say it myself, I was fast... but Charlie would beat me by five yards. Off the mark, he was gone like a jet."

Old teammates smile now when they say that Charlie didn't train all that hard, not in the sense of running 20 laps of a pitch, which was the done thing at the time. He sprinted, he took part in drills but mostly he was ball-in-hand, every chance he got. A sorcerer must have his wand.

With the ball, he was content.

"As long as Charlie was kicking a football and training with his friends, he was happy," says Donal O'Grady.

"He was a beautiful free-taker, he would curl the ball round with his right foot but he kicked with both feet equally well."

While his wife, Maureen, remembers him making the trek to the beaches of Donegal to pound the sand on occasion, Charlie's aversion to tough physical training was well-known.

"When we were training hard, he was often practising

shooting from all angles," says Gabriel Kelly. That wasn't unusual for a place-kicker, as Gene Cusack points out:

"I never remember him coming down to training that much, not early in the season anyway. But the free-taker and the goalkeeper got away with a lot at training in those days. There was a lot of grace extended to them."

Equipment was primitive. The football was heavier than it is now and had a protruding lace, which acted almost as a kicking tee. All frees were from the ground and the old ball seemed to cut through the wind.

Boots were rudimentary, although Gallagher took great care of his own. And of himself, too. When the big dogs in the full-back line started to snarl, Charlie was not keen to be their fresh meat.

"He was very light on his feet, he was always on his toes," says Ray Carolan. "But he rarely came into contact with anybody, he kept as far away from everybody as he could. He just kept moving. And backs tended to play in their positions that time; he'd get a fair bit of freedom and would score spectacular points.

"Charlie never got ordinary points. They were always *great* points. They curled around and around and over the bar."

As a result of his elusiveness and his ability to roll with the punches, he was rarely injured. He played countless matches in his career, often up to 50 in a season.

"I was sitting beside Charlie one day in the dressing-room and he was rubbing Wintergreen into his legs, it was the big thing at the time," remembers Kelly with a smile.

"I was surprised and I said to Charlie: 'Are you injured?'

"'I'm not,' he says.

"'Well, what are you putting the Wintergreen on for?'

"Says he: 'I want to smell like a footballer!' That was typical of him."

At the summit, where the air was thinnest, Gallagher needed one thing to survive: space. Granted that, he was deadly.

"Charlie bounced around the whole forward line," says Carolan. "He wanted to get into the space, he didn't want to be marked close. He'd be totally opposite to what forwards do today. When he got the ball, he took one look to see where the goals were and he had a go at it. That was the first thing in his head: 'I'll get a point from here.' Whereas now it's the last thing in most forwards' heads."

In that era, teams usually carried a couple of hatchet men whose job it was to scythe down the opposition's main threat: Gallagher. He got dog's abuse; took it, soaked it up and moved on.

"A lot of the time they would put a tight marker on Charlie because he was such a good scorer, and they wouldn't bother playing much football because he was the man to win a match for you," says O'Grady.

"But he would never retaliate. Never. He never threw a punch in his life."

Thrown into senior inter-county football as a 17-year-old, it was get tough or get off. Gallagher soon learned to roll with the punches and developed a knack for shipping hits and moving on.

"You'd seldom ever see him tossed or tripped, he could ride a tackle or a punch like Cassius Clay," says Sean Foy.

"Charlie's great skill was accurate kicking, from hand or ground, allied to extraordinary acceleration, balance and elusiveness," says Larry McCluskey.

"In tackles, he appeared to be always airborne, so that when he was hit — and many opposing players tried to hit Charlie Gallagher — he seemed to ride the tackle, not to lose balance, but go on to score. I don't remember him ever being injured or having to go off — at club or county level."

While Charlie tried to avoid contact where possible, heavy collisions were inevitable. Inter-county full-back lines were essentially shark-infested waters. When you took the plunge, some form of bite was inevitable.

Gallagher quickly learned how to take the punishment. Extraordinary footwork was his shield.

"He was the hardest fella to knock," says Phil Murray, who lined out alongside him in the Cavan forward line for the guts of a decade.

"Countless people tried to knock him, to hit him, but he was so stable and steady on his feet. He was like a ballerina."

Kelly remembers him "gathering himself up in a ball", when he came into contact with an opponent whose aim was to stop him and not much more.

If he drifted out from the goals in search of possession, Gallagher had a habit of gathering the ball and veering towards the wing. In that way, he could avoid the brutal intention of the centre, where play was congested and a couple of ruthless stoppers were sure to be patrolling. He found space along the sideline. He probably figured that he could score from there anyway.

"When he got the ball far out from goal, where every other fella would go straight for the goals, Charlie would head for the wing. And they used to be shouting: 'Lock hard, Charlie!'" says Foy.

That local refrain was commonly heard from the wits on the hill. The match was a Sunday ritual, a weekly carnival to provide some diversion for supporters. Lines like that were golden.

At an awards night in Crover House hotel in 1963, Ulster Council rep Andy O'Brien added his detail to that winking, local salute.

"In a game in Breffni Park, Charlie went off on one of his flashing solo runs along the sideline," he recounted. "A car-driver admirer of his, watching Charlie come dangerously near the corner flag, called out excitedly: 'Lock hard, Charlie boy!'"

In the house that Charlie constructed, though, frees were the foundation on which all else stood. He was guaranteed a few scoreable kicks every time he took the field and those built confidence. Put them over, hear the cheers, see the umpire's flag fluttering. It set him up for the next one, then the next. That familiar routine, magic in the mundane. He could score from the corner flag or from straight in front of the goals. Didn't matter. If the chance arose, he fancied it.

"He was a sheer opportunist," says Carolan.

"He'd be after getting one of these spectacular points and he'd come walking out and he'd say: 'What'd you think of that one, Carolan?!'

"But he didn't say it in a selfish or smart way, it was just the character that was in the individual."

Free-takers are manufactured by a process of repetition. In their construction, routine was the mortar. Three steps back, head down, strike it clean. Three steps back, head down, strike it clean...

"Charlie wasn't a man that would go out and catch a

ball or hold off a defender in a race to the ball, he hung in around the goals and if he got the ball, it was over the bar or under it," recalls Greenan, "and more than anything, he was deadly on frees."

Wherever he went, he would seek out a pitch and usually find a helper, a youngster, to collect the balls. And there he would work on his art; perfecting, honing. Kicking, kicking, kicking.

In UCD, Gallagher had some time on his hands and he put it to good use. There was a football field nearby: the sportsgrounds in Templeogue. His friend, James McCabe, of the '52 Cavan team, was teaching PE at the time in Clogher Road College around the corner in Crumlin.

Each week, Jim took the boys out for football and hurling practice. A pitch, some footballs, some help to gather them up — Gallagher never missed a Wednesday afternoon for two school terms.

One of the pupils under McCabe's tutelage was Seán Boylan, the future four-time All-Ireland-winning Meath senior manager. Boylan had attended Belvedere College and then completed two years in Clogher Road, where he was thrilled to be roped into assisting Gallagher with his kicking. Although only five years older, Gallagher was already a star.

"Jim McCabe and Charlie Gallagher would practise kicking and frees for around 40 minutes. We were enthralled by these two men and our job was to kick the ball back to them," remembers Boylan.

"If ever you wanted imprinted on you the value of practice and not wasting your time in training, that was it. All of the time they had to practice was used to correct what was going wrong and to put it right, there was no time wasted. They would practice until they would see it done right.

"It was a really interesting experience. Charlie was such an iconic free-taker. That black hair and the personality... and he was just a marvellous footballer. Charlie was an icon for so many years.

"I was privileged as a young man to see this — it was something I carried with me all through my life."

As did Gallagher. The skills he painstakingly acquired in his youth, he built his legend on.

SIX

The Postcard

In the bygone hierarchy of Ulster football counties, there was a certain social order. There were aristocrats, old money — that was Cavan.

If there was a middle class, it was occupied by Antrim and Monaghan, not that they were particularly upwardly mobile. As for the rest? They were penniless. Trespassers on a private estate, summarily dealt with once they were cornered.

An example? Cavan were the holders of the Ulster Championship in 1891 but then, due to dwindling interest, it lapsed for nine whole years and the county just claimed those titles as their own — all nine seasons, during which a ball was never kicked.

That artificially bumped their total of Ulster titles up from 34 to 43, at a time when Armagh, Down, Donegal, Derry, Tyrone and Fermanagh had one between them. It was like querying the difference in the figures after the decimal point on a billionaire's bank balance. Who was going to argue?

In the 27 years prior to 1955, Cavan had, including replays, appeared in 13 All-Ireland senior finals, winning five — including three in six glorious years between 1947 and '52.

The Polo Grounds win in '47 cast a shadow like no other. It was the pinnacle. A group of men from a rural place like Cavan flying to New York for an All-Ireland final was unthinkable. When the county had played Kerry in the 1925 All-Ireland semi-final — still within memory of several of the '47 team — the first word to reach Cavan Town, all the way from Tralee, was via carrier pigeon.

The Polo Grounds was massive and the county bathed in the afterglow — aided by the capture of the National League and the retention of Sam Maguire the following year. In 1949, they lost to Meath in a replay in the All-Ireland final but no sense of panic set in.

Veterinary student PJ Duke, the effervescent wing-back in '47, died aged 25 in 1950 from rheumatic fever (a fiercely-contested inter-faculty competition in UCD, in which Gallagher and his comrades would later compete, was named after him) and the '47-'48 team began to break up but still no sense of panic set in.

In '52, a side was cobbled together containing Tony Tighe, Mick Higgins, Simon Deignan and Phil 'The Gunner' Brady — the survivors of the earlier wins — alongside a host of new, unproven players. Led by Higgins, that ingenious, scheming centre half-forward, they scraped through Ulster, winning both the semi-final and final by a goal, then beat Cork by a point in the All-Ireland semi-final before defeating Meath in a replayed final.

It was a high-water mark for football in the county but, in hindsight, the All-Ireland win was papering over some cracks. The fault lines were there but it would take an earthquake to expose them.

The decline started immediately. Army commandant John Joe O'Reilly — leader, centre-back and a man who had gained almost mythical status — died aged 34 a month after the '52 win from a kidney ailment. The nation mourned. Coming so soon after Duke's passing, the county was reeling.

A year later, they had not recovered. Armagh, nobodies for decades, beat Cavan in the Ulster final — their first win in half a century.

By the end of the decade, Tyrone, Derry and Down would win their first-ever titles. It was a revolution that nobody in their wildest fantasies could have foreseen.

What made it worse was that they would all defeat Cavan in Ulster matches along the way.

"The main barrier to a northern team winning a senior All-Ireland title in football was psychological," wrote Maurice Hayes, the groundbreaking Down official of the time and architect of their success.

"One could only do one's best and put up a good show. And then there was Cavan, lying like a dragon in the path of any other Ulster county... The highest ambition any Ulster county could have was to beat Cavan once in a blue moon. That was their All-Ireland final. After that they had nothing left to achieve."

But in '53, Armagh managed it. "Which will hold out? Cavan's 'man for man' and 'catch and kick' or Armagh's speed and clever combination," the *Sunday Independent* had asked that morning.

The response was fairly emphatic. Armagh came into the Ulster final as massive underdogs but on a day of thunder and lightning in Casement Park, they lit up the championship with an upset win of 1-6 to 0-5 and went on to narrowly lose the All-Ireland final against Kerry.

There were more signs of decline, subtle but there all the same.

Key men were getting on, Tighe — a precocious, astonishingly gifted player who had won five Ulster SFC medals and two All-Irelands by the time he turned 21 — would be forced to retire at 27 with a back injury and, for one reason or another, there was a high turnover in personnel.

"That '52 team was really the last of the old guard," remembered Johnny Cusack, a tough, direct corner-forward on the '52 team.

"John Joe and Duke died and TP [O'Reilly] was gone and [Columba] McDyer was gone back to Donegal — he was on the '47 team only. They were gone off the team. Gunner was centre-field on the '47 and he was put back in full-back and the Maguires came on and Brian Reilly; Paddy Carolan and Seamus Hetherton; there came on a lot of new players in '52.

"All that was left from '49 was [Seamus] Morris, McCabe, the Gunner, [Victor] Sherlock, Higgins, Tighe... That was all that was left, the rest were all gone.

"John Joe Cassidy and Owen Roe McGovern were the subs from America that came on to the team after. They had Terry Sheridan, Eunan Tiernan and a brother of Deignan's and a whole heap of subs in America that never came on the team at all after, I don't know what happened.

"Connie Lynch was a sub that time, too, and didn't get to America and he played centre half-back for Meath then against us in '52; from '50 to '54 he played centre-half-back for Meath and was a great footballer."

In '54, normal order was restored, even without Higgins, who had packed it in that winter. Cavan saw off Armagh in the Ulster final, with young guns Brian Gallagher and Paddy Carolan, who scored 1-6 between them, playing "brilliantly", according to *The Anglo-Celt*.

In the All-Ireland semi-final, Cavan lost to eventual champions Meath by a point, 1-5 to 0-7, on a day when the Cavan forward line misfired.

The continued excellence of the Gunner, now a veteran, at full-back and the emergence of Jim McDonnell ("a force of nature, just an incredible player," according to James Brady) helped lift the team again in 1955, as did the return to the fold of Peter Donohoe.

The full-forward, who had been nicknamed the 'Babe Ruth of Gaelic football' after his performance in the Polo Grounds, had drifted from the scene in the intervening years, picking up a medal as an unused sub in '52 but had been otherwise forgotten.

Donohoe scored 0-8 of Cavan's 0-11 as they beat an improving Derry in the Ulster final and added another 0-9 in the drawn All-Ireland semi-final against Kerry.

On the same programme, Dublin and Mayo drew the other semi-final and in the prolonged build-up to the replays — a double-header on September 11th — the anticipation grew to a frenzy.

The replays were the lead story in *The Irish Press* the following morning.

"Excitement at fever pitch? That's putting it mildly," wrote John Healy.

"Nerves were red raw with excitement... at times it was unbearable."

For three men, it was. Two Cavan supporters and one Dublin follower dropped dead. John Maloney from Arva, a 64-year-old former Cavan footballer; James Monaghan, a shopkeeper from Poles aged 74 and 70-year-old Inchicore man Andrew O'Neill were all pronounced dead on admission to the Mater Hospital.

It was a bizarre, tragic denouement to a match which, once and for all, marked the end of an era for Cavan, who were dismantled, 4-7 to 0-5. The only shining light for the Ulster champions was the performance of McDonnell, who was magnificent, first at half-back and later midfield in a showing that cemented his place as one of the very best footballers in the game.

"The generous applause with which the crowd greeted McDonnell's efforts showed that every spectator present was well aware, despite what the scoreboard might say, that one Cavanman at least was unbeaten," said the *Press*, with the *Celt* describing McDonnell as "by far the best footballer of the day in either match".

Mick Dinneny, a Cavan hero of the groundbreaking 1933 and 1935 teams, sensed the danger. Dinneny had played for Cornafean, the dominant force in the county, but pointed out that there wasn't one player from the Reds on the Cavan team.

"The outlook," Mick said, "is extremely blue."

Another most famous, old Cavan footballer, Standish O'Grady, was in no doubt what was needed.

"I have come to the conclusion," he said, "that Cavan needs youth, especially in the forward line.

The selectors must have agreed. A couple of months later, in November, a card would arrive in Market Street, Cootehill. Charlie Gallagher's services were required by the Cavan senior football team for a challenge match, six weeks before his 18th birthday.

Young Gallagher couldn't have known, nor could anyone else for that matter, that the county's fortunes would plummet before they would ever come close to an All-Ireland semi-final again.

SEVEN

Old Money, New Order

There was a photograph, printed across four columns in *The Irish Press* on Monday, July 30th, 1956, the morning after the Ulster final, that brilliantly illustrates the changing of the guard.

It shows the Cavan goalmouth, at the town end of St Tiernach's Park in Clones, with an umpire reaching for a green flag and Tyrone goalscorer Donal Donnelly, wearing number 12, swaggering back to his position, his head cocked to the side as he surveys the crowd, who have encroached on the sideline.

On the left is Cavan goalkeeper Seamus Morris, helplessly panned out on the turf. To the right is full-forward Frank Higgins, airborne, as he follows up Donnelly's shot, lashing the ball into the roof of the net again in celebration.

And in the middle is a Tyrone supporter, who has broken clear of the rest and raced on to the pitch with an arm and all five fingers out-stretched seeking the hand of Donnelly, who is impervious.

That championship had started well for Cavan. At half-time in Casement Park in the quarter-final, they had been level with Antrim but moments after the restart, Charlie hit the net from 30 yards and Cavan went on to coast home, 3-15 to 2-4.

With brother Brian standing out in a new role at left half-back, Cavan had good reason to be confident about retaining the Ulster title and more — for one thing, in Charlie, they seemed to have found that new, young forward they had been seeking the year before.

"Star of the attack," said the *Celt*, "undoubtedly was Charlie Gallagher, who played a brilliant game throughout; indeed his conduct on the field and whole approach to the game could profitably be copied by both friend and foe alike."

Remarkably, later that evening, the Gallaghers played a second match. A large crowd from Cootehill had journeyed north to take in the Cavan game and then a challenge match against Antrim champions O'Donovan Rossa, who included in their ranks Down star Kevin Mussen. The Celtics won it, 1-11 to 3-2.

The semi-final was against Armagh, Cavan winning by 1-9 to 1-5 in Castleblayney, during which Brian Gallagher's goal from a 50-yard free-kick — clipping the underside of the crossbar on its way — set Cavan on their way in a match that "had practically everything except good, clean football."

"Any boxing coach looking for potential championship material would have found this game rewarding," wrote Tom Cryan — who later found fame covering the fight game, particularly Barry McGuigan — in the *Press*.

And then came the final and Cavan's world came crashing down.

¶ ¶ ¶ ¶

"Under the high hill that makes a natural banking for the football field in Clones, thousands of Tyrone people went wild with joy yesterday — and with good reason," began a colour piece in the *Press*.

"For the great barrier had been leaped. The fifteen blue-jerseyed men who stand between any Ulster team and Croke Park had been beaten....

"Every Tyrone man secretly but fearfully hoped for victory. The man who sat beside me said he hadn't slept a wink in a week."

Cavan had been destroyed, the Red Hands swatting them like flies. Tyrone were ahead by a point at half-time and as torrential rain fell in the second half, they dominated, eventually winning by 3-5 to 0-4.

"At one stage," read the report in *The Ulster Herald*, "I saw Phil Brady and Seamus Morris exchange glances and Morris shrugged his shoulders in a questioning attitude, as much as to say 'What is really wrong?'"

In the *Press*, Cryan was scathing.

"Brian Gallagher, one of Cavan's leading lights against Armagh, was probably the biggest disappointment of the day. Neither he nor his brother, Charlie, at half-forward, were anything like the force they were in Castleblayney."

It was an earth-shattering result. Tyrone had never won an Ulster senior or junior title before; not even a McKenna Cup. That they managed it in such style and against Cavan — "Cavan routed as never before," screamed one headline — made it almost unthinkable.

The Tyroneman's Association in New York later brought the team across the water for two weeks, feting them at banquets and dinners and organising matches in Gaelic Park and the Polo Grounds. Another box ticked, another infringement on to a domain that had been Cavan's and Cavan's alone.

"We thought we were gods," Tyrone's 19-year-old captain, Jody O'Neill, would recall.

"I'd been to Dublin, I'd been to Belfast [but] I didn't know what the world was like."

O'Neill had a vivid memory of a Monday morning in 1946, the day after Cavan had hockeyed his home county in a championship match by 8-13 to 2-3. Jim Devlin, the legendary Tyrone full-back who was later murdered during the Troubles in 1974, was at the counter in his grocery shop and asked O'Neill and two friends what they had thought of the previous afternoon's match.

"He reached over the counter and grabbed me by the pullover until we were nearly nose to nose and he said 'O'Neill, as long as you play football or watch football, remember this: forwards win matches'."

Nine years on and O'Neill, still a schoolboy, was playing alongside his hero. Tyrone ventured south for the All-Ireland semi-final against Galway with a spring in their steps with the rousing words of Phil 'The Gunner' Brady, who had spoken to them in the dressing-room after the game about doing the province proud, still ringing in their airs.

Devlin was to mark the iconic Frank Stockwell and, the night before, in Barry's Hotel, told anyone who would listen that he would hold the Tuam man scoreless. Within earshot was Galway's Sean Purcell, a future Team of the Century full-forward, who asked Devlin if he would care to put a wager on it.

A fiver was produced and Purcell matched it. The next day, Stockwell failed to score but in the raucous aftermath of Galway's 0-8 to 0-6 win, the bet was forgotten. Decades later, at an event in Dungannon, Purcell would chuckle that he still had Devlin's five-pound note at home, framed.

For the Gallaghers, it marked the end of a horrible few months. In May, their brother, Fr Frank, had taken ill in England.

Frank and Charlie, despite the age difference, were close. Frank had been ordained a priest a couple of years earlier and was posted to a parish in the town of Longton, near Stoke-On-Trent. He became sick, a kidney complaint, and came home to recuperate but he would never return.

On May 5th, the family borrowed a television set and Frank was well enough to watch the FA Cup final — Manchester City beat Birmingham City, the game in which the winners' German goalkeeper Bert Trautmann broke his neck and played on.

But his condition drastically worsened. Two days later, at just 30, Rev Francis De Sales Gallagher — named after the patron saint of writers and the deaf — breathed his last.

His youngest brother took the death badly. The funeral was one of the largest ever seen in the area, attended by 56 priests and members of the Cavan team, including Mick Higgins and The Gunner Brady.

Gallagher would never forget his brother. "Dad wasn't religious but he would always say to me 'Frank will be looking out for you'," remembers Charlie's daughter, Louise.

¶ ¶ ¶ ¶

Few then knew but 1947 — the year of Cavan's greatest triumph — would mark the beginning of the end of their stranglehold in Ulster. All-Ireland titles in 1937 and

'38 and an All-Ireland final appearance by a team featuring Tom Maguire and a 16-year-old Jim McDonnell in '52 aside, Cavan had flopped in the minor grade as the northern teams grew in strength.

On September 14, 1947, as Cavan were preparing for their senior final in the Polo Grounds, Tyrone defeated Mayo by a point to bring the All-Ireland minor title to the Six Counties for the first time. The following year, they retained it against Dublin and the year after that, Armagh won it for the first time, beating another aristocrat in Kerry.

The northern teams were on the rise.

"Cavan were getting it tight enough in Ulster from '46," recalled Johnny Cusack.

"Antrim and Armagh and Tyrone and those teams were coming up. From 1927 on till the mid-forties, it was only a matter of walking out for the Ulster final but that was starting to change."

That year — 1946 — was a particularly successful one for the 'other' Ulster counties, with Down, from nowhere, winning an All-Ireland junior title, St Pat's College from Armagh claiming the Hogan Cup and Antrim stunning Cavan in the Ulster senior final.

But the biggest change of all came a year later, by way of a decision which had nothing to do with football. Winston Churchill had been shunted out power and the Labour government brought forward a radical wave of progressive, liberal reforms. For the first time, there would be a welfare state.

The Butler Act in England and Wales in 1944 and the Education (Scotland) Act of 1945 were followed by the 1947 Education Act in Northern Ireland, introduced by the Stormont Government amid fierce Orange Order and populist Protestant opposition. In increasing funding to the Catholic school sector, the legislation, according to Professor Graham Walker of Queens University, "was of a piece with the social reform ethos of the times, and the determination to build a more just society out of the trauma of war".

"The Act," it has been documented, "required the building of secondary schools, including top quality sports facilities, for pupils up to the age of 15 and the employment of specialised PE teachers to instruct them. For the first time Gaelic games were included on the course syllabus for students and the game enjoyed equal status with other activities."

Suddenly, Catholic children had access not only to free secondary education but to expert coaching in Gaelic football when they were at school. By the mid-to-late 1950s, a generation of educated Northern nationalists were reaching adulthood and beginning to enrol in third level education in large numbers for the first time. While they had not been completely liberated, the nationalist population of the North had been given the means to further themselves.

Gaelic football was the sporting pursuit overwhelmingly favoured by this section of society and as the game quickly began to boom and so did the interest levels; in 1961, a year before RTÉ made the leap in the south, the BBC would become the first station to televise a Gaelic football match.

So, when 1957 dawned, Cavan had been deposed and were now posed with a challenge, within Ulster, the likes of which they had never faced before and for which they were totally unprepared. The storm was coming and unsurprisingly for Cavan, things would get much worse before they got better.

¶ ¶ ¶ ¶

In 1957, Tyrone retained their Ulster title. Cavan had a patchy National League campaign, with Brian Gallagher their best player and Charlie, despite some injury problems — a rare occurrence in his career — nailing down a place at wing-half-forward.

In April, they lost the league semi-final to Kerry by a point at Croke Park but had a good warm-up for the championship a fortnight later when beating Tyrone; Charlie enjoyed his "best game to date for Cavan" in a one-point win to mark the opening of new pitch in Tempo.

Monaghan were comfortably beaten, 1-12 to 1-5, in the Ulster quarter-final but Cavan were stunned by another of the *nouveau riche* northern teams, Derry, in the semi-final at Dungannon.

The *Celt* bemoaned the extra time added on by the referee, with the only possible explanation, they reckoned, having been a delay while the ball was retrieved after Gallagher "kicked it into the next field while attempting a score".

It mattered little. Sean O'Connell, Gallagher's future teammate with Ulster and Ballerin, kicked the winner and Derry held on, 1-9 to 1-8. For only the second time in 35 years and the first since 1938, Cavan would not take their place in the Ulster final.

Derry, who had only had an organised county board since 1933 — by which time Cavan held the province in a vice-like grip and had already put in place a county grounds — reached their first Ulster final in 1955, losing to Cavan. Now they were back and would face Tyrone in an all-Six Counties clash.

The times they were a-changing.

¶ ¶ ¶ ¶

In '58, it took Cavan three games to get over Monaghan in the first round. Making hard work of Monaghan was notable in that, while the Farneymen had won the previous year's All-Ireland Junior Championship, they hadn't beaten Cavan in the Senior Championship in 28 years.

They drew first day out in Clones in a match the *Celt* reckoned "must rank high on the list of the worst games of football played under a championship tag", where "dog rough, useless, mulish play was the order of the day".

In the *Independent*, legendary writer John D Hickey commented that "for the most part, the ball was merely of secondary importance. The players had worn themselves out in the orgy of ankle-tapping, elbow-slinging and jersey pulling and the hundred and one tricks which all the too-old, the unfit and the sub-standard footballers know and use when the opponent is getting the better of things".

Poet and playwright Tom MacIntyre, saved two Monaghan penalties to force a replay, which wasn't much better; the sides drawing 1-5 apiece at Breffni Park on a day when the Tavey brothers, John and Paddy, from Donaghmoyne lined out for opposing sides. Extra time, as was the norm, was not played because the referee had retreated to the dressing room to get away from "a mob, hundreds-strong".

The third game was fixed for Casement Park on a Sunday evening and this time Cavan clicked, building up a 0-8 to 0-1 half-time lead and eventually winning 0-14 to 1-6, with Charlie "re-establishing himself in no uncertain manner, scoring four great points from play".

On the same afternoon, Down came out of ether to topple Tyrone by 1-9 to 0-2. With the champions gone, Cavan could have fancied their chances but Derry lay in wait again the following Sunday.

Charlie landed the first two scores of the Derry game — he would finish with 2-3 — but what was described as "a tragedy of errors" befell Cavan, with Brian Gallagher hitting the post with a penalty; Seamus Conaty striking the crossbar and, in the end, Derry — inspired by Player of the Year in waiting Jim McKeever — running out 4-7 to 3-6 winners.

"I came on to the team in '45 and didn't win an Ulster title for 14 seasons, until 1958," remembered Roddy Gribbin, Derry's player-manager that year.

"That's why I appreciated it so much. I played for that long and Cavan would usually pip us to the post, every year."

The Derrymen would go on to beat Down in the Ulster senior final. History was made. In the curtain-raiser, however, Down gained some consolation, as their "crafty forwards", ominously made hay in hammering Cavan by 3-9 to 3-1. It was the Down's maiden Ulster minor title.

The underdogs were biting back, hard. And for Cavan, there was more what that came from.

Another Derryman, Paddy MacFlynn, had been part of the GAA's official delegation that had gone to the Polo Grounds. He knew the power and the majesty of Cavan and he knew things were changing, too.

"The blue jerseys of Cavan... There was nothing in Ulster to even compete with them," he said.

"Antrim were the first team to really put it up to them in the mid-'40s. Then Down came..."

¶ ¶ ¶ ¶

Ulster final day was and is a pilgrimage, the masses of Ulster Gaels descending on Mecca, usually Clones.

The Ulster final was generally played on the third Sunday in July. The sun shone. Supporters left early to get a run at the day.

"It's a fair, a festival, a Fleadh," MacIntyre would write a few decades later, after attending the latest instalment as a supporter.

"In the crush and scramble I saw people I hadn't seen for decades. The fair resembles a big wedding, a grand funeral... There should be a painter present, I muttered."

When MacIntyre was playing in those matches, the event was much the same. Every nook and cranny of the town was crammed. The colour remains the same; only the colours change.

In Clones, the locals showed an entrepreneurial spirit. There were what was called a 'meat tea' to be bought, from makeshift stalls in alleyways and entries — sustenance for the journey home.

Fleeting moments can change the course of a sporting lifetime. A goal here, a tackle there. A split second decision.

When Tyrone lifted The Anglo-Celt Cup for the first time in '57, after dismantling Cavan and dashing the hopes of 19-year-old Charlie Gallagher, their captain Jody

O'Neill, the same age, had brought the old trophy down the town, through the throng, to The Creighton Hotel on the bottom of Fermanagh Street. There he met his father and the old man's friends.

"There was an archway underneath the hotel and there were hay bales. My father was there with a group of Coalisland people and I brought the cup down and of course they wanted to take a drink out of it.

"And one of the boys said to me 'come on, Jody, you have to take a drink'. I looked over at my father and he said 'whatever you like son'. I didn't take it..."

Until the late 1950s, many travelled by train. Clones was a vital railway hub and that helped build the tradition whereby St Tiernach's Park would host the biggest games. By the end of the decade, though, roads had improved and cars were becoming more commonplace. Railways, north and south, were closing down; the sleepers destined to rot in the ground and be overgrown by weeds.

With personal ownership of cars increasing, inter-county teams could streamline their preparations, meeting at central locations to train during the week. On and off the field, the late 1950s was a time of radical change.

Footballers of Cavan had come to see the Ulster final, and lifting the cup at the end of it, as their birthright. But by the dawn of 1959, Charlie had been a first-choice senior footballer for three championships and had yet to pick up an Ulster medal; his only final appearance ended in a chastening 10-point defeat. Charlie was the anointed one, the forward who was destined to keep the colours of the tribe flying for another generation. It wasn't supposed to be like this.

Gallagher was making his name with UCD and had

been carving up defences in the green and white hoops of Cootehill since he was a boy but in the royal blue and white of Cavan, progress had stalled.

By the dawn of 1959, alterations had been made to the landscape.

Cavan, though, eased to a handy 2-9 to 0-4 win over Donegal in their championship opener in Ballybofey. A last-minute Brian Gallagher point earned a draw against Armagh next time out in a match the referee accidentally blew up three minutes early.

Cavan won the replay, 1-9 to 1-7, with the Gallaghers scoring 0-3 each and James Brady the remainder.

"To Charlie Gallagher," wrote Hickey, "goes a special word of praise for what he accomplished, though pitted against a man of the calibre of John McKnight."

On the other side of the draw, Down had confirmed their dominance over Tyrone by trouncing them in a replay. The Mourne men's rise had been well-flagged and Cavan were wary.

The *Celt* sports editor, PJ O'Neill, however, could only see a win for the traditional heavyweights. O'Neill, a Wexford native and brother of Polo Grounds referee Martin, had revolutionised the sports pages of the newspaper, in common with what was going on around the country. Interest in Gaelic games was at an unprecedented level — a record 90,000 would attend the following year's All-Ireland football final — and colour GAA magazines were flying off shelves.

Newspapers were responding; even the staunchly unionist Belfast papers were beginning to carry limited GAA coverage.

O'Neill, who would introduce the Sports Page Arena

section to the *Celt* — effectively an opinion column and soapbox for fans with something to get off their chest — was not one to shy away from calling it as he saw it.

He commented that "if tradition counted for everything, then the match is as good as over" but noted the "deadly lethargy" that had plagued Cavan teams in the previous handful of championships.

"Cavan have had a lean time in the football world," he wrote, "and the up and coming northern teams have gained in confidence with Cavan's downfall."

One had to go back to 1915, when Cavan won the title after a seven-year gap, for the last comparable famine, he said. But he expected Cavan to win and restore some pride.

The enthusiasm still comes through in chairman TP O'Reilly's quote in the same article:

"The spirit is excellent and we are definitely out to take the title back to Cavan."

O'Reilly's old All-Ireland winning teammates Hughie O'Reilly and Joe Stafford, along with Higgins, were part of the backroom team and Cavan moved their training base from Virginia to Bailieborough, where they prepared rigorously.

The Evening Herald, which carried a photo of Gallagher, expected Down to mount a strong challenge but, in common with the other papers, did not foresee them claiming a first provincial senior title.

In the end, the *Celt*'s headline the following week — "Too bad to be true" — told its own tale as Down won their first Ulster title by an astonishing 2-16 to 0-7.

Peadar O'Brien in the *Press* described Down's victory as "thoroughly deserved, utterly convincing and wonderfully popular". It was Down's first Ulster title and some of their supporters among the 30,000-strong crowd climbed the goalposts, O'Brien recorded, in celebration, placing a Down flag at the peak.

As a metaphor, it could not have been more fitting. In sweltering heat, Cavan's status as a footballing power seemed to have evaporated while Down, tracksuited and in black shorts (both firsts for a GAA team) tore them to shreds.

At half-time, Down led by 1-10 to 0-2. By the end, the Gallaghers had scored all of Cavan's total but it mattered little. "Ninety per cent of the Cavan players," the *Celt* added, comically, "were literally stuck to the ground."

For Down, even though they would lose the subsequent All-Ireland semi-final to Galway, things were just starting. The magnificent Sean O'Neill, at 19, had won an Ulster medal at the first time of trying. The 1960s beckoned and promised to be glorious.

On the undercard, the Cavan minors defeated Antrim in the Ulster final. A glimmer of hope, maybe, but the golden age now seemed further away than ever.

Winter was coming and on Christmas Day, Charlie would turn 22. For the first 17 summers of his life, Cavan had won 16 Ulster titles. Since had come on to the team, they had won none.

He and Brian, Tom Maguire, James Brady and Noel O'Reilly, as usual, shared a car for the trip back to Dublin. On this occasion, it was a sombre journey while, up the road, the party was only starting, in every sense.

"I was fortunate in 1959," O'Neill would recall, "because I got on the end of a rocket that just took off."

For Cavan, things would never be the same again.

"Down gave us a hiding in the Ulster final and went on to play Galway in Croke Park in the All-Ireland semi-final," remembers Gabriel Kelly, who attended that match.

"I remember coming out of Croke Park and a fella said: 'Oh, that Down team is a flash in the pan, you'll never hear of them again.' How wrong he was."

Charlie poses as a ventriloquist's dummy, sitting on the knee of friend and neighbour Kevin Carney, at a Scouts concert in the late 1940s.

Charlie as a small child outside the family home in Market St, Cootehill.

Above: The St Patrick's College, Cavan team photographed before the 1954 MacRory Cup final. Charlie is in the back row, fifth from left.

Right: At 16, Charlie (front, right) made the Ulster Colleges senior football team in June 1954. He and his teammates are pictured at the front door of St Patrick's College, the famed football academy.

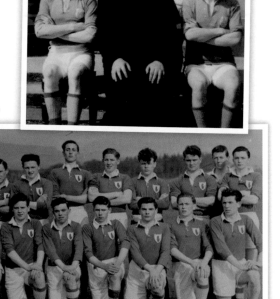

Charlie (back row, extreme right) lining out with the Ulster Colleges football team against Connacht in Sligo in 1955.

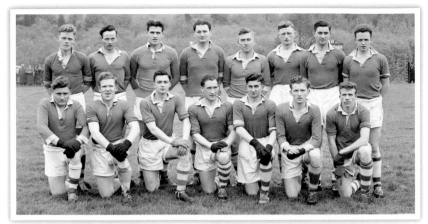

The Cavan team pictured before a NFL match against Meath in Kingscourt in 1958. Charlie is third from left in the front row. Also pictured are James Brady (second from left, front row) and Jim McDonnell (extreme left, back row).

Charlie (extreme left) in action against Longford in the National League in 1959.

Charlie (third from left, back row) with his Cootehill Celtic team-mates after beating Gowna in the 1960 Cavan JFC semi-final.

Above: Charlie with his parents on his graduation day in 1961.
Left: Fr Frank Gallagher, Charlie's eldest brother, who died in 1956 aged 30.

Right: The photo, printed in the *Evening Herald*, which cost Charlie a season's football – Charlie (second from right, front row) with the team of dental students who won a soccer tournament in UCD.

The Cavan team before they played Roscommon in the 1962 All-Ireland SFC semi-final at Croke Park. Charlie is fifth from right, back row.

Above: The Cavan travelling party board a plane for London and Wembley Stadium in 1963. Charlie is at the entrance to the plane, on the right.

Right: Charlie, Gabriel Kelly and Tony Morris in a taxi from Wembley Stadium after winning the magnificent O'Gorman Cup.

The Cavan squad who played Kerry in the 1964 All-Ireland SFC semi-final at Croke Park. Gallagher is on the extreme left in the front row, beside his friend Frankie Kennedy.

Praise of player

Sir—I would be pleased if you published a little tribute to Ireland's top scorer, Charlie Gallagher.

P.H.

IF I had money, time and tools,
  A monument I'd build,
I'd paint it bright in blue and
  white,
  And place it in Cootehill.

* * *

I'd count the points that
  Charlie got;
  On bronze I'd place them all;
And stand it high in his home
  town,
  Where he first played a ball.

* * *

In his game against the cham-
  pions
  Their back line he did draw.
He played the ball but not the
  man,
  And won the praise of all.

* * *

You talk of the speed of
  Leydon,
  Or your straight-shooting
  Long;
But I'll shout about our Charlie
  And in praise sing my song.

* * *

With speed and dash he played
  the game,
  And well controlled the ball;
And not one man could stop
  his speed
  That played him with football.

Meeting a native American in New York in 1964 (above) and with Galway hurler Joe Salmon on the same trip (below). Left: A poem published in the *Evening Herald* in 1964.

Gallagher is third from left in the front row at a training camp in Kilnacrott in 1964. Mick Higgins, extreme right, wears the priest's mitre.

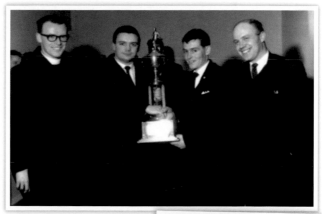

Presenting awards in Newtownbutler, Co Fermanagh with Fr Iggy McQuillan in 1964.

Polo Grounds comrades and key figures in the 1960s TP O'Reilly and Mick Higgins. Right: Cootehill and Cavan legend Hughie O'Reilly.

Charlie (front, centre) captained Cavan to a win over Kerry in the National League at Croke Park in 1966.
Left: The Anglo-Celt, Wembley and McKenna Cups were all held by Charlie, as captain, at one point in 1967.
Below: The coin toss in a deserted Croke Park.

EIGHT

The Ban

Sunday morning, November 6th, 1960. Cootehill are to play Cross in the Junior Championship final. Sean Foy, the impish team trainer and local barber, attends early Mass and heads for home.

On Market St, outside his own front door, stands a glowering Hughie O'Reilly, the three-time All-Ireland winning manager.

"Call a meeting," he told Foy, disappearing back inside, "in Connolly's pub in half an hour and get as many off the committee as you can to come to it."

So, Foy got to work and rounded up half a dozen committee men.

"We landed in. 'What's this about?' Hugh Murray says.

"'Well, I'll show you now,' says Hughie and he pulled *The Evening Herald* out of his pocket and there was a photograph of UCD after winning a soccer competition and Charlie Gallagher standing proudly in the middle of them."

As evidence goes, it was damning. Eleven soccer players and one official and, in front of them, a cup. "The Dental team with the Independent Cup after they had beaten the Mater in the final of the Hospitals' Soccer Cup at Bird Avenue yesterday," read the caption.

There were no names but none were needed. Kneeling, second from the right in the front row, was

Charlie Gallagher, that unmistakable grin beaming off the page.

The committee members looked at each other.

"'Ah', I think it was Andy Brady, says, 'not many people read the *Herald*, they won't see it.'

The iron man was not for turning.

"'I don't care who sees it,' says Hughie, 'he'll not be playing and that's it.'"

The "dreaded man", as Foy described him, had spoken. Charlie had been caught playing the foreign game. Suspension was inevitable.

It had taken Cootehill three games to get past Gowna in the semi-final of the Junior Championship. For the second replay, they brought Brian Gallagher home from England and it made the difference; the crucial score coming when "Brian sent Charlie storming through the middle for a magnificent goal".

Dr Brian was home again that afternoon for the game against Cross and the Celtics expected a win. In the end, even without Charlie — left out in anticipation of his suspension and possibly the club's own should they have fielded him — they managed it but it was a filthy game at Breffni Park.

Tempers spilled over at the end with "a Cootehill player felled in one of two fistic efforts".

"Nature in the raw had its fling," noted the *Celt* of fans encroaching on to the pitch.

"When a spectator rushes on to the field with his blood up and his brains behind him to kick a player lying on the ground, he deserves to be lined up against the end wall and shot."

Eight days later, at a county board meeting, came the

verdict on the Bird Avenue matter. The chairman of the county board, solicitor TP O'Reilly, had won All-Irelands under Hughie's management in 1947 and '48 and was a stickler for the rules.

The first case heard on the evening was that of Tom White, a former Cavan player. It wouldn't have filled the Cootehill delegation with confidence.

The chairman himself was bringing a similar 'foreign sports' case against White and even though the board had accepted White's evidence, it wasn't enough. A public cleansing was needed, a renouncement of this grievous sin.

White was to be given a chance to publish a mitigating letter in the *Celt*, stating that he was no longer engaged in these games — before any penalty was imposed. The player had written to the letter to the county board but gave no authority to have it published. Verdict? Six months.

As for Gallagher, his was an open and shut case.

"A lot has been said from time to time about photographs and other proofs but this player's photograph had appeared in an evening paper dated November 5th as playing with a soccer team," stated TP.

"That is good enough for me," he said, imposing the suspension for six months to run from November 4th, the day of the match and commending Cootehill for not playing him in the junior final.

So, the county board, desperate to beat Down and reclaim past glories, had taken the unusual step of banning their best forward. That Christmas Day, Gallagher turned 23. He wouldn't kick a ball again until May.

¶ ¶ ¶ ¶

By the time Gallagher returned to the side for the McKenna Cup, Cavan were in disarray. They had lost all five matches played during his suspension and when the championship rolled around, he was stuck in the middle of his final exams in UCD.

In early June, he graduated and, at the ceremony on a Saturday afternoon, he was approached by Barney Cully, an Arva man and a princely full-back in the glory days of the '40s for county and province. Cully, a staunch Cavanman, ran a successful dentistry practice in Derry city and saw an opportunity. "You're coming to work for me," he told Gallagher.

Cully had broken new ground in Derry. A superb footballer in his own days who had played in the 1943 All-Ireland final and missed out on the Polo Grounds trip — due to being suspended for playing rugby — Cully was not afraid to take a chance on anything, not least giving a job to a young graduate.

"It sounds like my father," says Cully's son, John.

"He would head-hunt. Dad was a real innovator and divergent thinker. He had stocks in London way before anyone knew what that was, he was the first Catholic to buy a house in a Protestant area in Derry. He got a Protestant doctor to buy it for him. That sort of stuff."

Cully's practice was on Clarendon Street, a mostly Protestant enclave in the heart of the city, which was mainly Catholic. The street was lined with doctors' and dentists' practices. Against the backdrop of the civil rights movement, the political rise of John Hume and the downtrodden Nationalist working class, the Catholic middle class was beginning to assert itself.

But there remained huge deprivation in the city. "Going

to school," says Cully, "all of my classmates, all of their fathers would have been unemployed. All of them. I went to boarding school in Newbridge later and was with kids whose parents had a few bob. It was a big change from the streets of Derry I had walked as a young fella. Up there, it was poverty. Poverty."

¶ ¶ ¶ ¶

So, the following Monday morning, Charlie reported for duty in Derry.

The chat in the clinic that morning would surely have been about the previous afternoon's disastrous showing by the county footballers. Cavan had been humbled in the sunshine in Lurgan, losing by 2-7 to 0-8 to Armagh and failing to score a single point from play. It was the first time the county had lost in the first round of the Ulster Championship since 1915. It was, all agreed, rock bottom.

When Down went on to stroll to a second All-Ireland title in succession, the depression in Cavan football circles began to be replaced by a desperation.

By winning an Ulster title, Down had proven themselves to be successors to Cavan but Tyrone and Derry — and even Antrim back in '46 — had done that, too. It wasn't unprecedented.

Winning an All-Ireland, though, and in such style, was new.

Down the road in Cavan, the feeling was mutual. Nothing would ever be the same. The sense of identity not just of the footballers but of an entire county was wrapped up in the sport — Cavan were, or had been, the kings of

Ulster. That was just what they did and now it was taken away from them. Down would have to be stopped.

Cavan became obsessed with beating them.

"The Ulster final in 1959 and the league final in 1960/61 were massive wins for Down because Cavan were the dominant force in Ulster for decades," says Colm McAlarney, who would break into the Down side while still a minor in 1966.

"When I think back on it now, from a Cavan perspective, they must have always looked upon us with great respect but also with a great deal of anger, too, because we must have seemed to be usurpers of their proud tradition and they were very keen to put manners on us."

Later on, there would be a mutual respect there, for sure, and firm friendships in many cases but on the field, it was a fierce rivalry.

"There was a great familiarity between Cavan and Down," says Ray Carolan.

"There would usually be six or seven Cavan fellas playing with Ulster [for the inter-provincial Railway Cup] and six or seven from Down. The reality was that we played more football with the Down guys than we did against them. We knew them very well and if you got a chance to meet them in an Ulster final, you were just waiting to get at them."

So, in '62, whatever it took to beat Down was worth exploring. Cavan had won the Ulster junior title 18 times but had turned their noses up at it for a few years. That would change; a county junior team was assembled and, for the first time ever, went into training. And there were a couple of game-changers that no-one could have predicted; a raft of new talent from St Pat's and an ace in the pack. With Gallagher having missed out on the Senior Championship the previous year, he was eligible to play.

Before their opening game in Donegal Town on the day after St Patrick's Day, the *Celt* noted that Gallagher while "not available for last year's Senior Championship outing against Armagh" has been "Cavan's leading forward for years".

Against a Donegal side that included Cootehill man Tony Keyes — then a Garda stationed in Dungloe — and future All-Ireland-winning manager Brian McEniff, Gallagher was handed the captaincy. Word travelled slowly back then; when the teams lined up for the parade behind the De La Salle School brass band from Ballyshannon, some Donegal fans in the "exceptionally large" crowd were outraged on spotting Gallagher.

But, despite the objections, the Cavan captain was eligible and landed all of Cavan's six points in a 1-6 to 0-7 win, despite appearing, according to one report, well off full fitness.

"There was uproar, the Donegal crowd threw stones at us. We had a good team without Charlie but with him we had an exceptional team. But he was as much a showman on the junior team as with the seniors and he, maybe, rubbed it in!" laughs Frankie Kennedy.

Phil 'Lightning' Murray, who would go on to be an outstanding forward at senior level, was a sub on that occasion and remembers the barrage of abuse Gallagher took after the match.

"Coming out of the game, I remember the Donegal crowd attacked him. Why? I suppose because he was the star man on the day and was a county senior player of renown but here he was playing junior football. They were very sore about it."

Antrim were up next and Gallagher bagged 0-10, with just one point coming from a free, in a nine-point win which sent the county back into the Ulster junior final for the first time since 1958. The following week, the senior team, with Gallagher at full-forward, beat Derry in the McKenna Cup semi-final.

Down, inevitably, were the opponents in the junior final and a crowd of 3,000 turned up at Carrickmacross to see Cavan win by 0-8 to 0-7. After a slow start, Gallagher, who "led the line with characteristic spirit and dash", kicked his side into the lead for the first time with 10 minutes to go and kicked his fifth point, the winner, in the dying seconds.

The previous week, the *Celt* had carried two prominent stories on its front page. One was a report on how the Bishop of Clogher, the Most Rev Dr O'Callaghan, had raged, at a confirmation ceremony, against proposed new longer drinking hours in pubs. Beside it, above the fold, was a story about 40 gallons of poteen being discovered on a mountain in west Cavan. The bishop's crozier may have almost reached out of the page but the wildness would not be tamed.

But on that week of the junior final, the main photo on the front was of Charlie Gallagher, carrying a few pounds alright; in an over-sized jersey with sleeves rolled up and his jet-black fringe falling down above his right eye, smiling and shaking hands with a five-year-old fan, himself bedecked in dickie-bow and striped jacket, his hair in an identical style.

The kid was named Sean Fox, the caption said, and he

was presenting Charlie with a shiny, new gold cup named after his late uncle, a priest. By the time the All-Ireland junior semi-final against Meath came around, however, the junior team would be decimated, Higgins having ransacked it and taken the best for his senior side, rendering them ineligible. But the shadow competition had served its purpose. The All-Ireland champions now lay in wait.

NINE

Brothers In Arms

In 2014, *The Irish Independent* carried a special supplement detailing each county's greatest XV of the previous fifty years. Alongside it was some brief commentary on each team's fortunes.

"It remains a significant anomaly," the paper noted, "in the storied history of Cavan football that they never won an All-Ireland in the 1960s."

To this day, it is a source of regret and wonder in equal measure. Cavan could beat any and every team on a given day and did but they didn't beat the right teams on the right day. It slipped from their grasp.

"If you look at the team of the '60s, most fellas on the team played inter-county football for a long number of years," Ray Carolan says.

"A lot of guys who came on in '62 stayed around for years. The basis of the team was the same."

While, in actual fact, only Carolan, Tom Lynch, Gabriel Kelly and Charlie Gallagher remained until 1969, picking up four Ulster medals on the way, Carolan was right in that the 1960s line-up was, aside from the goalkeeper and full-back positions, mostly a settled one.

From 1962 on, the nucleus of a strong cast of characters was beginning to be formed. That quartet would be at the heart of it.

By the middle of the decade, Kelly was already commonly regarded as one of the greatest corner-backs the sport had seen. Born in Cavan, he moved to Mayo as a teenager for work and won a Connacht minor medal and a county Senior Championship before coming back to his home county.

In 2011, he would be named on the *Irish Independent*'s Unsung Heroes team — the best XV never to win an All-Ireland medal — at left corner-back. He was a lion-hearted defender who was in his prime in the middle of the 1960s.

"If somebody went up to Gabriel Kelly and said he was playing somebody brilliant he'd say 'who is he? Never heard of him'," smiles Carolan.

"His attitude was, the ball comes in, I'll get it, it doesn't matter how good he is. It was positivity, a lot of them had that."

Lynch played most of his football at centre half-back and midfield.

For the first half of the decade, the team was led by Jim McDonnell. The Bunnoe man had burst on to the scene in 1955 and was a force of nature, usually at wing-back.

"It was fairly tough football, I mean if you went down you were hurt. You didn't go down except you were hurt and you'd be kind of ashamed to be put down, you wanted to get up as quickly as you could, even though you mightn't be feeling that good," he said.

McDonnell was not old but he was viewed as a veteran, the natural leader of the team. He had come through the ranks in St Pat's and UCD, a tried and tested path for Cavan players of his era, and, like Gallagher, had rubbed shoulders with the best players in the country in college circles and knew he could mix it, and more.

"At that time I went to UCD in '54 and I played with all the Kerry fellas there," McDonnell recalled.

"The UCD team that time, there were 15 county men and the subs were all county men as well, so I got to meet a lot of them, Jerome O'Shea, Sean Murphy, Paudie Sheehy, Jim Brosnan, all of those guys were there in UCD at the time so it helped us a lot. We saw that they weren't supermen. They were very ordinary fellas. I realised that."

In goals on the 1962 team was Sean Óg Flood, who had won an All-Ireland medal with Louth in 1957. PJ McCaffrey was full-back, a teak tough west Cavanman.

The half-back line was brilliant. McDonnell was on the wing, Tom Maguire was in the centre and Tony Morris on the other flank.

Both were inter-provincial players; Maguire, a natural leader and a big presence in the dressing-room, would win five Railway Cup medals. Morris was tough as nails and a big game player with the temperament to match.

"Tony Morris was the finest cut of a man ever came into my shop," smiled Foy.

At midfield was Carolan, an extraordinary man. At 15, he had been an unused sub on the 1959 minor team and would go on to star in successive MacRory Cup-winning teams.

His strength, fielding ability and resilience marked him out as one of the best in the country from day one. By the mid-1960s, he would come to be regarded as the pre-eminent midfielder in the country.

Beside him, Lynch was a fantastic athlete who could field and play ball, too. Up front, Gallagher was the star, even then, but James Brady was a terrific foil, a brawny, intelligent inside forward with an eye for goal. Centre-forward Hugh Barney O'Donoghue, a pharmacist from Virginia, was awesome in the air and Jimmy Stafford, nephew of Polo Grounds hero Joe, was young, energetic and fearless.

It was the best Cavan team in years and would only get better. The back-line, and the ball-winning ability of Carolan and Lynch, was the foundation.

"McDonnell was sharp, a really good footballer, a genuine player — I remember in training, nobody would want to mark him," recalls Lynch.

TP O'Reilly, a solicitor from Ballyconnell, was chairman and an obsessive Cavanman. Football was everything and Cavan football the only thing.

"We played a match in Casement Park," remembers Carolan, "and I remember we stopped in Armagh for a meal and TP got up on the table before the game, and it all laid out, to give a speech. He was so excited."

TP and Mick Higgins, the manager, were close, having played together for county and province throughout the 1940s. Higgins was a superstar, a three-time All-Ireland winner, softly-spoken but hard as a coffin nail. A Garda Sergeant, Mick — born on the day Michael Collins was shot, in New York — was a doggie man in his spare time, tending to his greyhounds with affection.

But inside the velvet glove was an iron fist. Higgins, a brilliant, scheming centre-forward who was adored for his modesty and cool demeanour, was just as determined as O'Reilly was to restore Cavan to past glories.

¶ ¶ ¶ ¶

First up were Armagh. In a stormy match — the second half took almost an hour to complete after a pitch invasion by incensed visiting fans — a haul of 1-3 from James Brady helped Cavan win by 3-8 to 2-2.

When the stewards cleared the pitch, many fans remained on the sidelines and the closing stages were played out in a surreal atmosphere; with the result beyond doubt, some players "lost interest" while others settled some scores. Regardless, Cavan won, although Gallagher was subdued, scoring just one point.

Antrim were next and Cavan were slightly concerned, with McDonnell and O'Donoghue injured. They suffered a further blow before throw-in when Gallagher cried off with a throat infection but a great goal from Seamus McMahon early in the second half steered them home, 1-6 to 0-5, with Carolan and Kelly "lording it".

All-conquering Down were next.

¶ ¶ ¶ ¶

The match took place on July 28th in Casement Park. Cavan had momentum behind them, having promoted the young, energetic junior players and with the McKenna Cup — normally, if not a trinket, then certainly a distant second-best — safely secured.

What made that latter success important was who they beat en route to the final against Armagh — Down.

"We had taken hammerings from Down in '59 and '60 and '61," recalled McDonnell.

"There was one particular game I remember in Newry in the McKenna Cup around about that time. Of course, Down didn't put out their full team. That time you could put on as many subs as you wanted and by the time it was nearly over, they had their full team on! We went down, mad to get at them of course. We beat them anyway and it was a great boost, at the time we thought we couldn't beat them. It was around '61."

¶ ¶ ¶ ¶

On the eve of the Ulster final, Vincent Pilkington, a football-mad 14-year-old, was running an errand to a bar in Cootehill.

"My uncle Joe used to send me down for two bottles of stout in Packie Eddie Lynch's in Church Street," recalls Pilkington.

"The price was 10 pence a bottle. Joe said to me 'go down and get that and see would you see Charlie.'

"So I went down on my bike and bejaysus, who did I see coming only Arthur 'Doc' McCabe and Charlie and Brian Gallagher in the back of Packie Eddie's. I was 10 foot tall going back on my bike. I was only 14 and you wouldn't get into a bar that time till you were 18 but just to see them. When Charlie came from Derry, I can't describe what a big deal it was."

¶ ¶ ¶ ¶

Entering the final, the holders were red hot favourites but Cavan had cause for optimism.

"That Cavan are in with a chance is not just an assumption based on a certainty that some day, sooner or later, the champions will slip up and that day might well be Sunday," wrote PJ O'Neill in the *Celt*.

"One can't ignore the fact that since Cavan took positive steps to get back on the football map early in the year, their stock has been following a steady upward trend."

Winning the Ulster junior title and the McKenna Cup, O'Neill reckoned, were priceless boosts.

"These were successes of no little significance since the competitions have produced the players who will line out on Sunday."

Down had been on a tour to the United States, ostensibly spreading the Gaelic football gospel. There was a sense that they were vulnerable and Cavan tore into them. Their young players were fearless.

Gallagher, by now 24, was desperate to make up for lost time. As McDonnell led the team in the parade, before a record Ulster final attendance of 40,000, Gallagher was next, socks up, hair oiled. Within a minute of the throw-in, he had fired over the opening point from 50 yards. The tone was set.

In the end, it was easier than anyone expected. James Brady took a pass from Stafford and slammed home after 15 minutes and the former, making his first start in the Senior Championship (he wouldn't turn 19 until the following October) pounced for another first-half goal as Cavan went in at half-time winning by 2-3 to 0-4.

Walking off at the break, a smiling Brady turned to Stafford.

"That was a great pass you gave me," he said, "you'd hardly have another one?"

As it turned out, it was Stafford himself who came up with the third.

The Down half-forward line was said to be the greatest in history but Cavan dominated that sector throughout. McDonnell thwarted Sean O'Neill, Maguire blotted out

Jim McCartan and Morris was magnificent in holding Paddy Doherty scoreless.

"Tony Morris was a great footballer too, he was probably one of the top backs in the country," says Lynch.

"Tony had a dry sense of humour. He was playing on Paddy Doherty in 1962. We were going out for the second half and I happened to be going out with him, and I said to him, 'Jesus you're doing a good job on Doherty, keep it up and we'll win this'.

"And he called me back and he said 'who did you say yer man was?'"

Doherty, of course, was a genius, the man Gallagher rated as the best he had seen. As for Charlie himself, he wore number fourteen but roamed all over the forward line, finishing with four points.

In roasting heat, Lynch and, in particular, Carolan, came of age, controlling the midfield in a revelatory performance. Down tried five different markers on Carolan; nothing worked.

"Down were heroes at the time," Carolan recalled.

"I was playing in the middle of the field in the final and caught the first ball and came down with it and I never saw anybody. And I got such a fright I nearly dropped the ball!

"And the second ball came out and I went up and caught it and I sort of looked around to see where the hell were these fellas. And then you start to think, 'Jesus, I'm better than these fellas'."

By the time referee John Dowling of Offaly, whose wedding took place the next day, sounded the final whistle, Cavan had won by 3-6 to 0-5. It's impossible to overstate just what the win meant to Cavan. This one ran deep. Pride was restored.

"That Ulster final in '62 was a landmark day for Cavan because Down were admired the length and breadth of Ireland," says James Brady, whose goal set them on their way.

"Down were *the* team then," says Morris.

"If they had beat us, they'd have won the All-Ireland. But it was a mighty day, a real hot day in Belfast and we just tore into them."

In the *Press*, Mick Dunne described the result as "a facile victory, all the sweeter because it amply avenged the humiliation of that defeat in Clones three years ago."

Cavan were the champions again and the summer now opened up before them. For the players, though, life went on. Carolan, described in one newspaper as "already the best midfielder in Cavan, Ulster and maybe even Ireland", was quickly brought back down to earth.

"I was after leaving St Pat's and I was working in a summer job in the Co-Op in Mullagh," he remembers.

"We beat Down and on the Monday morning at half nine I was above between Kells and Dunshaughlin unloading six or eight tons of coal off a lorry.

"They were ten-stone bags of coal and you had to heel them off and bring back the bags. There was a fella who was a cousin of mine with me and there was was a fella, a Mayo man who lived in Meath, and he began to talk about the match in Casement Park and he mentioned my name as this good young fella who was playing.

"And the fella pointed at me heeling the back of coal and said 'that's the gasun you're talking about there'. There was no big deal about it."

That week, the *Celt* carried a photo on the front page

of McDonnell receiving the cup from Ulster Council president Paddy McFlynn. To his right are McCaffrey and Stafford and, between them, grinning broadly and straining to get into the shot, TP O'Reilly, BL.

It had been announced that the Anglo-Celt Cup was to be replaced with a new version. The winners would retain the old cup; McDonnell keeps it to this day.

Down were left to lick their wounds and rue what might have been. It is widely accepted that had they beaten Cavan, they would probably have won a third All-Ireland in succession.

"We had gone to the United States, which might not have been the brightest idea in the world," Maurice Hayes would reflect.

"But we were driven to it because we had refused before. We were asked to go to areas outside of New York and their season was May and June.

"We thought we could do it. The mistake we made was we were back home and people were saying we were living it up in New York and not training. We were training away, but we needed a rest after playing two matches a week for weeks.

"We should have seen the signs. It would have been nice to be a three-in-a-row team."

¶ ¶ ¶ ¶

In Connacht, there had been a surprise. Roscommon scored 1-1 in the final minute to snatch the Nestor Cup by a point against Galway.

Cavan, suddenly, were the hottest of favourites to make a first All-Ireland final in 10 years.

The Irish Press sent Mick Dunne to Virginia to cover a training session and the vibes were positive.

McDonnell was bullish about his team's chances.

"If Down had won the Ulster title they'd have been at least 3/1 on to win this game so we must have a 50/50 chance or better. Granted we get our share of luck, we'll win."

Higgins, always prescient, told the reporter the result "hangs on our forwards and whether they can take enough of their chances".

Standing in earshot, Brady heard his manager's comment. "It's a pity we don't have him on Sunday," he smiled.

Higgins' concerns had some basis. The previous Sunday, Cavan — at full-strength bar Flood — had been lucky to draw with Carlow in the Grounds Tournament at Finglas, the forwards shooting 20 wides.

"Granted, they showed not a trace of nerves in the Ulster final," predicted Dunne, "where Carolan struck me as one of the greatest midfield prospects I've seen for a long time and Stafford took his scores coolly and confidently.

"But Croke Park can be a different matter, especially when pitted against older and more physically mature opponents. Such is Cavan's wastage in attack that they must get a more liberal service of the ball from half-back and midfield than many another side needs."

And so it came to pass. A few days later, in the big one, Cavan collapsed. The attack misfired, badly, and a middling Roscommon team fell over the line, 1-8 to 1-6.

McDonnell, who added to his legendary status when he took over from goalkeeper Flood, who had been knocked out, and saved a penalty, knew it was one that got away.

"We went out against a mediocre enough Roscommon team in the semi-final and got beaten by two points, having missed 12 frees. That was one we should have won really," he said.

Cavan shot 18 wides, with Gallagher and Con Smith "worst of all", with some of their efforts from placed balls "astonishingly wide of the mark".

"In all post-mortems that will surely be held in Cavan, none can ignore the inescapable truth — the Breffni men kicked themselves out of this championship," wrote Dunne, who quoted a disappointed Kelly as saying simply "they took their chances, we didn't, that's why we lost."

The Evening Herald nailed it in a punchy three-word headline: "Cavan's misses fatal."

For Carolan, it was a sobering afternoon. In hindsight, bringing so many up from the junior side was a leap too far and after the highs of Casement, they came undone against seasoned, stubborn if limited opposition.

"We were too naive. We couldn't adapt," remembered Carolan.

"What happened against Roscommon was that we were totally inexperienced. There's a big hype from winning an Ulster Championship and going into an All Ireland semi-final. We were kind of depending on the more experienced fellas on the team, fellas like Jim McDonnell, Tom Maguire and Con Smith and as far I can gather some of them didn't play well.

"We were at midfield on two big fellas, John Kelly and Bernie Kyne — I've never forgotten their names — and they were obviously told to break the ball in the middle of the field. It was the first time that I came up against fellas who lay on your shoulders and used the fist to try to break the ball.

"I think I got caught in the sense that i wasn't wise enough to adapt the tactics. A lot of the fellas were probably young and were the same."

On the way home, TP called into Higgins' home in Virginia.

"It was a poor Roscommon team. I remember there was terrible depression that night," said TP's Garrett, then a 14-year-old engrossed in football who would, within five years, be on the team himself.

"We were at Higgins' for a while. Mick mightn't show it as much as my father would show it. He would be totally gutted. Life wasn't worth living. Because it'd be almost a child-like excitement beforehand."

What made it worse was that there were no excuses. Cavan should have won and they blew it.

"Without a doubt," says Brady. "Jesus, without a doubt, we should have beat Roscommon."

Morris summed it up.

"We should have beat Roscommon, Roscommon were no good of a team."

¶ ¶ ¶ ¶

The week before the Roscommon game, the juniors had played Cork in their All-Ireland semi-final. The line-out was unrecognisable from the Ulster final, with eight players having stepped up to the seniors.

In the build up to their semi-finals, the seniors and the shadow squad had sparred in training.

"The juniors beat the seniors in a challenge match. That's a fact. And there was skin and hair flying," recalls Frankie Kennedy.

Kennedy came on at wing-back as Cavan trounced the Rebels, 3-10 to 1-7, before a massive crowd in Breffni Park.

"Imagine taking that many players off an Ulster-winning junior team and moving them up to senior and the remainder of what was left was still good enough to make the final and run it to one point.

"That's the standard there was in Cavan — the talent that was there within the county."

While there was devastation at the manner of the loss to Roscommon, the bones of an exceptionally good team was in place.

TEN

Flight From The Land

The Cavan players returned to their clubs and licked their wounds. A few weeks after the Roscommon loss, Cootehill qualified for the Senior Championship final with a 1-9 to 1-8 win over Bailieborough.

In the dying seconds, Brian Gallagher was fouled and his brother took the resulting penalty. It struck the crossbar and Charlie gathered the rebound and found the net.

However, the game wasn't entirely over. Cootehill fielded Jimmy O'Donnell, a brilliant centre half-forward, who had recently arrived in the town and would go on to be a big player with the county.

But the Shamrocks objected, having got wind that O'Donnell had lined out with Leitrim earlier in the year and was thus illegal. While the wrangle was going on in the boardroom, and the threat of a ban hung over the club, the county team took no chances and left Gallagher off for the opening games of the 1962/63 season.

He returned to the side as a sub against Kerry in the Grounds Tournament in late October but it was "plain as a pike-staff" that he was not on his game.

A week later, he came on as a sub again, scoring a goal in a narrow National League loss to Mayo in atrocious conditions in Westport and returned to start for the win over Sligo, scoring 0-5.

In March, he scored another goal in a win over Leitrim

— a game that had originally been called off after the death of a spectator. By now, a couple more of the 1962 junior team had broken through, including Phil 'Lightning' Murray, the gifted corner-forward from Cavan Gaels, and the Mayo native and defender Donal O'Grady.

After finishing his Leaving Cert in Ballina, O'Grady had enrolled in Ballyhaise Agricultural College, where another defender on the '62 junior side, Shay Given's uncle Ambrose Given from Donegal, was also studying. Higgins had got wind of him and made the approach.

"Mayo didn't bother with me after minor and Mick Higgins asked me would I sign on for the Cavan juniors, they had won the Ulster junior and half the team was gone because they had played for the seniors. They were playing Cork in the All-Ireland semi-final in Breffni Park and he asked me would I play and I did... They were stuck with me then for a few years," says O'Grady.

By the following season, O'Grady was on the seniors. An informal approach from Mayo had been rejected. O'Grady was happy with Cavan and was proving a great addition to the side.

"I wouldn't do it [switch allegiances back]. And Mayo never beat us in my time. I came in as a stranger, if you like, but it didn't matter after one or two games When you take the blows for each other and become friends with a bunch of fellas, it doesn't matter where you come from."

Down were on the radar again in a play-off for a trip to Wembley. Cavan were gunning for it and made sure they were at full-strength; selecting Tom Lynch, Tony Morris and John Joe O'Reilly, who had been chosen to play with the gardaí in an annual fixture against the army on the same day.

"TP and Higgins were mad to beat Down because Down had beaten Cavan a few times. We had to play off with them then in my first year to go on the trip to Wembley and I was sure we had had it won. I remember James McCartan and Tom Maguire were swinging punches at each other at the end of the match. But walking off the field, I was told it was a draw and we had to play them again in Castleblayney."

After that draw in Carrickmacross (1-7 apiece), Gallagher finally found his stride again in a National League play-off against O'Grady's home county at Croker in late March, which Cavan won by 3-11 to 1-7, "making a hare of Connacht full-back Vincent Nally".

"A top-class display by Cavan's full-forward Charlie Gallagher highlighted this dreary play-off," began Peadar O'Brien's report in the *Press*.

"He fooled the Mayo defence time and again, scored a goal and four points and had a hand in almost all of the other Cavan scores."

But Cavan's form was up and down. Meath beat them by three points in the divisional final at Drogheda in a filthy match. The Royals' tactics were slated in the *Celt*, prompting a letter to the sports desk, penned under the sobriquet 'Dún an Rí (Kingscourt) Gael' but, it was noted, posted with a Kells postmark.

"Only once," the disgruntled fan wrote, "did a Meath player raise his fist and that was in the first half when Quinn struck Charlie Gallagher."

Tom Lynch, midfield that day, remembers well the treatment Gallagher endured.

"Quinn destroyed him physically, I mean he belted him all over the place. Anyway, Meath beat us and we went into the hotel after the game and I looked around and there was the bould Charlie and Martin Quinn above at the bar. Charlie *couldn't* hold a grudge."

Next time out, in a match for the Corn na Cásca (Easter Cup) in Croke Park played as a curtain-raiser to the Railway Cup hurling final, Gallagher scored 1-6 in a 1-9 to 0-11 win over Dublin.

Weekend dates were becoming scarce and the Ulster Council made the decision that Cavan's McKenna Cup semi-final with Down would double up as the replay of the Wembley tie and Cavan rose to the occasion, winning by 1-13 to 3-4 in Castleblayney, with Gallagher notching 0-7.

A week later, they were off to London.

¶ ¶ ¶ ¶

On his visit to Ireland in June of '63, John F Kennedy had referenced the problem of emigration, which was decimating rural Ireland.

'Most countries send out oil or iron, steel or gold, or some other crop," he famously said, "but Ireland has had only one export and that is its people.'

In 1950s Ireland, agriculture still accounted for approximately two-fifths of the working population "but the small farm rural economy, especially in the west of Ireland, was in an irreversible decline".

Ireland was the only country in Europe, apart from East Germany, to see a population decline in that decade; it has been estimated that half of all Irish people born in the 1930s and three out of every five children who grew up in the '50s emigrated at some stage, the vast majority to Britain.

By 1966, RTÉ would run a special news item on emigration across the Irish sea.

"Mass at the beginning of Sunday and dancing at the other end," began the script.

"In their relaxation, that's one way of recognising the Irish, which is not always in the bottle as some would have us believe. In places like this, they create their own little piece of Ireland."

Wages were higher — a barman in the west of Ireland might earn £1 a week, a quarter of what barmen were making, on average, in England — and the rate of emigration hinged on educational attainment, which was low in rural areas.

By 1956, a Commission on Emigration would note that it had become "a part of the generally accepted pattern of life".

The Commission also identified an inferior standard of living in some rural areas, which "appear dull, drab, monotonous, backward and lonely" to many young people.

In 1965, Damien Hannan of the ESRI and a group of researchers interviewed 556 young people, mostly in their mid-to-late teens, in Cavan Town and its environs. His work, Rural Exodus, became a classic of the genre.

Hannan found that a lack of opportunities for people with a certain level of training or education was a key factor in driving them away. They felt they had no option but to leave, with 36 per cent stating that they definitely intended to emigrate and 40 per cent unsure.

In 1968, Hannan would follow up and find that most of those he had spoken to three years earlier had gone through with their intentions, one way or another. Interestingly, the majority of Hannan's respondents said that they would have preferred to stay at home and almost all had exhausted the possibility of finding work in their own area.

Cavan, a very rural area, was hit harder than most. Between 1946 and 1956, it had the sixth highest rate of depopulation of the 26 counties. And while others steadied and then began to recover in the '60s, Cavan's population continued to fall — between 1966 and 1971, it was one of only six counties to see a decline in population, a trend which would not be righted until the late 1990s.

The decimation in rural numbers was inevitably having an effect on Gaelic games. Writing in Gaelic Sport magazine, renowned GAA journalist Raymond Smith identified the threat posed by emigration to traditionally strong, rural GAA counties.

While, by the 1950s, farmers operating at county level were almost a thing of the past ("Big men who tilled the soil in the day and played football or hurling in the evenings dominated county teams in the early years of the GAA... Some of the greatest sides were formed of farmers and farm labourers."), their number was falling at club level, too, by dint of the fact that there were simply less of them.

And farmers had always backboned country clubs.

Ironically, for those left behind, the landscape was growing brighter. By the early-to-mid 1960s, the economy was picking up — Gross National Product increased by four per cent in 1963 — and society in general was becoming more affluent. There were more and more cars on the road and average wages had increased, even with the flight from the land continuing. While there was an increased focus on foreign investment, in crude terms, it could be argued, for the people who chose to stay at home, there was more to go around.

"The young," wrote Smith, "seeing opportunities for better pay and conditions and better opportunities for leisure and recreation and regular hours either left for the big towns and cities or emigrated to England."

Paul Rouse says that the country was transforming quicker than is often believed.

"Ireland was beginning to change in the fifties and the sixties. Everyone talks about Ireland being a backwater in the fifties and that's a bit unfair. There is a thing that people sometimes portray and it doesn't hold true: that living in Ireland in the fifties was almost like living in the fifteenth century.

"You do have to acknowledge that there was huge conservatism around a whole load of other things but at that time, there was money beginning to come into the country — in the sixties, at least."

In England, the GAA was a bedrock of the Irish community. A crowd of 42,000 turned out to see Cavan play Kerry, the largest attendance ever recorded at a Gaelic football match played outside of Ireland, paying 21/- for the stand and 5/- for terrace tickets.

The visiting players were treated like royalty, with old and not-so-old Cavan players and supporters desperate to meet up and get a taste of home. Donal Kelly, who had captained Bailieborough to the county title against Cootehill six years earlier, was there, as was Eamon O'Reilly from Belturbet, who played a few games up front alongside Gallagher a couple of years earlier.

Kevin Blessing, a Cootehill man, who also played with

Gallagher for a while and lined out with the Cavan minors — alongside Morris, Kennedy, Murray and others — in the 1959 All-Ireland final, called to the hotel on Friday evening, having finished his day's work at an insurance firm.

Blessing, young, educated and ambitious, was typical of the brain drain. There were countless like him from Cavan alone. He was, by then, playing his club football with London's Shamrocks, where the manager was Fr Seamus Hetherton, an All-Ireland winner with Cavan 11 years earlier.

The team was billeted at the Royal Hotel in Russell Square. After a banquet in the Irish Centre in Camden Square on the Friday night, they enjoyed some sight-seeing on Saturday. Sunday was game day and Cavan were ready for Kerry.

"Sure I thought I was going to heaven. It was my first time in England," says O'Grady. "It was just great fun."

In the match, Cavan were eight points up early on, with Gallagher "rampant", but Kerry, featuring the legendary Mick O'Connell, who had arrived from New York on the Friday, pulled it back and won by five.

That evening, the party was entertained at a function in the stadium attended by Irish Ambassador to London, GC Cremin, and Minister for Social Welfare Kevin Boland, who had thrown in the ball.

Some of the group made the trip to the dogs at White City, where Cassius Clay — in town for his fight with Henry Cooper a few weeks later — was in attendance, drumming up publicity and soaking up the comic boos from the crowd.

"A character is this Cassius," wrote PJ O'Neill in the

Celt, "but a charming one I found when my escort introduced me to him after the din had died down. 'He falls in five,' he said, and I was picking no argument with him because whatever about some of the footballers I had seen in action earlier, this was one fit and dedicated man."

The Cavan party returned on Monday and, with an Ulster title to defend, got back to work at their training base in Virginia that week. Three days later, JFK landed in Ireland.

¶ ¶ ¶ ¶

A couple of weeks after their return, Gallagher made the short trip from Derry City to Ballinascreen for Cavan's first defence of the Ulster title. The venue was something of a fortress but Cavan brushed Derry aside. Gallagher repeated his habit of opening the scoring, this time with a 40-metre point from the wing, and finished with 0-7. James Brady added 1-3 as Cavan led by 3-9 to 1-6 with 10 minutes to go before Derry rallied to leave four in it at the finish.

Donegal were next and fancied the task. They were back in their first Ulster semi-final since 1957 with a new young side, backboned by three survivors of six years earlier in goalkeeper Seamus Hoare, midfielder Sean Ferriter and wing-back Sean O'Donnell, a friend and sometime drinking buddy of Gallagher's.

Gallagher scored the first point but it would be his last. Donegal were leading by 2-3 to 0-4 at half-time and eventually ran out 4-6 to 0-5 winners to reach their first Ulster final.

"For Donegal," reckoned the *Celt*, "this victory was

nothing more difficult than taking candy from kids." For Cavan, it was humiliation.

"The centre stage spot which Charlie has occupied for so long was usurped by a new star," reckoned Eoin McQuillan in *The Irish News*. "Donegal's Sean Ferriter, a tall, rangy centre half-forward, cut paths of glory for himself through the leaden-footed Cavan defence."

The Ulster final took place in Breffni Park, where Down sliced Donegal open.

Down were well beaten in the All-Ireland semi-final by Dublin. For Cavan, it was back to square one.

Oh, and Cooper? He fell in five, alright.

ELEVEN

'What Did You Think Of That, Frankie?'

In September 1963, Charlie — by now well-established with Barney Cully and making good money — took a holiday in Spain. While he was away, Cavan played Donegal in the McKenna Cup final and were hammered, 2-8 to 0-5. It was Donegal's first win in the competition and another milestone in the rise of the 'other' Ulster teams.

Charlie returned to the team for league games wins over Westmeath and Leitrim and a loss to Longford, totting up 3-13 over the three matches, which meant that by the year's end, he had finished as the second highest-scorer in the country with 6-53 in 14 matches. The winner, Bernie O'Callaghan of Kerry (who had scored 1-8 against Cavan in Wembley), came in with 9-53 in two more matches.

Yet in January, Gallagher was omitted from the Ulster team for the Railway Cup, which prompted outrage in Cavan. A letter-writer to *The Evening Herald* demanded answers.

"I don't ever remember seeing a better or cleaner footballer in all my years watching Gaelic football. His omission from the team is inexplicable in the extreme."

At the county convention, TP lashed out about it, too, expressing his "disgust" at Gallagher having only been included on the subs. Higgins, he said, was an Ulster selector but was "a lone voice crying in the wilderness" on this one.

Cavan, he said, had endured a dreadful year, surrendering the Ulster title in senior and junior and the McKenna Cup. Even the minors had been trounced by Fermanagh.

"But," he concluded, "the darkest hour is always the hour before the dawn."

And so it would prove.

¶ ¶ ¶ ¶

Gallagher's superb form continued. Five points against Sligo and 0-8 versus Meath brought his total to 4-33 for the National League, making him by far the leading scorer in the country. He would end up coming on in the Railway Cup final at Croke Park, too; kicking a late point in a three-point win over Leinster alongside Kelly, Maguire and McDonnell.

Charlie was hot property and, early in the New Year, word reached Cavan that his exploits had been recognised.

Just seven footballers and hurlers nationwide were to be selected to line out in Gaelic Park, New York, in the John F Kennedy Memorial Games, a field day designed to raise money for the recently-deceased hero of Irish-America. Speculation was rife about who would get the call.

"Make no mistake about it," wrote Peadar O'Brien in the *Press*, a newspaper Gallagher religiously sifted through each Monday morning, "a trans-Atlantic visit to see the lights of Broadway and the many wonders of the

New World is regarded by many to be of greater value than an All-Ireland medal."

Along with Des Foley (Dublin), Joe Lennon (Down), Seamus Murphy (Kerry), Packie McGarty (Leitrim), Gerry O'Malley (Roscommon) and hurlers Joe Salmon (Galway) and Billy Rackard (Wexford), the group flew to the Big Apple for the April 19th event.

It was Gallagher's first time in New York — he had never been in the country before — and he instantly took to it, and it to him. Americans like their sports stars to carry themselves with a little swagger and Irish exiles, desperate for a slice of home, were dazzled.

The organiser was a Kerryman, John 'Kerry' O'Donnell, a fabulously wealthy publican who had taken the lease on Gaelic Park when it was at an all-time low in 1945. It was a smart move. A rising tide after the war lifted all boats and John Kerry surfed the wave.

Gaelic Park became an Irish oasis in the city, with five matches each Sunday during the season and, more importantly for the owner, 35 taps were needed to keep them in drink.

The GAA in the city was something of a banana republic and the Kerrymen its benevolent dictator, holding enormous sway in GAA circles at home, too, and regularly quoted in the Irish press. He had the power and the means to bring players and officials to the States and that gave him huge status at a time when such jollies were rare in cash-strapped Ireland.

So, word arrived in February of the April extravaganza and soon the players were on their way. It was a carnival atmosphere, Gallagher at the heart of it. The group took in the sights and smells of the city.

Seventeen years had passed since Cavan had won the All-Ireland final there; since Cavan player John Wilson had been bowled over by its intoxicating mood.

"The city was full of lights, the shops were full of food... the bars all had televisions. The whole city carried an air of prosperity; everything was just go, go, go."

While Ireland had not changed all that much in the intervening years, and rural Ireland even less so, across the Atlantic, it felt like anything was possible. Two months earlier, a 22-year-old, mouthy heavyweight called Cassius Clay had "shook up the world" by toppling Sonny Liston and the Beatles had landed in JFK, altering pop culture forever. In the week the players arrived, the Liverpudlians occupied the top five places in the Billboard charts.

A couple of weeks after the Irishmen returned home, President Lyndon Johnson would first reveal his plans for a Great Society — an unprecedented liberalisation programme which aimed to wipe out poverty and racial injustice. It felt like the dawn of time.

New York was growing rapidly. The first of the Baby Boomers were reaching adulthood and the futuristic World's Fair — featuring space-age jet-packs, colour television and Michealangelo's Pieta, which had been borrowed from the Vatican — opened at Flushing Meadows during the Irish party's stay.

The Irishmen lapped it up. Gallagher was the star turn, wowing fans everywhere he went. He was photographed, in sunglasses, with a Native American; in full regalia, grinning broadly. In another picture, he's standing in front of a restaurant with Salmon, wearing a broad smile. It was a happy time. Some of the best players in the land, feted like kings on the footballing holiday of a lifetime.

Kennedy had been assassinated six months earlier and the nation hadn't fully absorbed the shock. Along the east coast, sports organisers threw themselves into fundraising; two days before the event in Gaelic Park, Robert Kennedy had attended a benefit baseball match at Fenway Park in Boston.

A crowd of 11,000 turned up for the GAA event, with Gallagher lining out for his home county against Leitrim, who, inspired by McGarty — then, and now, regarded as the county's greatest player — won by 1-9 to 1-8. Gallagher scored all of Cavan's eight points, four in each half.

The football, though, was an after-thought. Charlie roomed with O'Malley, whom he had played Sigerson football against, and, years later, loved to recount the story about his new buddy opening his suitcase, packed by his wife, to find it brimful of Aran sweaters, far from ideal for the New York sun.

"Gerry O'Malley and Charlie Gallagher were chalk and cheese but became amazingly close on the trip. O'Malley was very serious, religious and quiet; Charlie was devil-may-care..." recalled McGarty.

"Gallagher was always winding Gerry up and saying if they ever met in a match that he would destroy him, which drove O'Malley mad. They were a pantomime. In private, Charlie admitted that he would have hated to have to play O'Malley.

"Down's Joe Lennon was on that trip, too. He had written a book about Gaelic football at the time and he brought loads out with him and sold them wherever he went. One day Charlie went up to O'Malley and said, 'You know what, I'm going to write my own book about football.'

"'Really? And I suppose we're going to see Gallagher on the front cover in full flight with the ball?'"

"No chance," Charlie assured him. The cover photo would be a glamorous blonde. McGarty never forgot it. The brashness and the devilment.

On May 1st, the group boarded flight 102B and flew home, John 'Kerry' accompanying them ahead of his latest joust with the powers-that-be in Croke Park. Waiting for Charlie at Dublin airport was a parking ticket — in the excitement heading off, he had parked his car illegally and owed a hefty £3. What could he do only smile?

¶ ¶ ¶ ¶

Cavan lost by 1-8 to 0-7 to Down in the league semi-final on a day when the forwards failed to shine but the following week, Gallagher struck 1-4 as they beat Monaghan well in the McKenna Cup, a tally which brought him back to the top of the national scorers list.

Down, though, were waiting in the wings again and Gallagher's five points couldn't stop them inflicting another defeat, by 1-8 to 1-6, in the McKenna Cup semi-final in Kingscourt, after which PJ O'Neill, in the *Celt*, decried the forwards' "diabolical habit of 'all stand still' whenever Charlie Gallagher gets the ball."

"If we could only get them to move," he wrote. "They don't look so hot as statues."

Cavan were busy on the challenge match circuit in the lead-up to the Ulster Championship opener against Derry, beating All-Ireland champions Galway to mark the opening of a new pitch in Cornafean. Gallagher chipped in with 0-8.

On June 14th, Cavan took on Derry at Breffni Park. Their preparations were a shambles, the match was delayed by half an hour as the visitors waited for players to arrive. In the end, they fielded without three of those selected and Cavan tore them open, winning by 3-9 to 2-3, with the luxury of a dismal 22 wides. Gallagher finished top-scorer with 0-6.

Donegal were next, in the semi-final at Irvinestown. "Gallagher's accuracy the deciding factor" read the headline on Dermot Gilleece's report in the *Press*, which told its own story.

"If Donegal had had Gallagher, the result could just as easily have gone the other way," reckoned the reporter, who highlighted the corner-forward's six-point haul and his pass for Tom Lynch's goal as key.

"Gallagher showed how frees should be taken, no matter the angle," reckoned the *Independent*.

Down remained the market-leaders in innovation and had spawned a thousand copycats. Before the championship, Donegal, desperate for a breakthrough, had abandoned their traditional green and saffron jerseys in preference for a red strip, presumably in unspoken deference to the Ulster holders.

The change "was expected to lend mythical stature to the appearance of the team," reckoned O'Neill, who used both Cavan and his native Wexford vernacular when he added that it was "little use in looking like men and playing like a lock of chaps."

Cavan won easily enough at Irvinestown, 1-9 to 0-7, and Down, for the third time in a few months, awaited. As always, Cavan were desperate to beat them.

The previous year, Down made history when they

became the first GAA team to fly to a match in their own country. Cavan aped that, too, when they jetted south to play Cork on July 5th, beating the Rebels by 1-12 to 1-6 in a challenge in which Gallagher bagged 1-7, 1-4 from play.

Not long home from the States, the Cavan talisman had never been fitter. He had begun to organise an Ulster All-Star team, made up mainly of his footballing friends from around the province, who would rock up in mid-week at various venues and take on club selections. The proceeds from the gate went to charity — after meals and a few drinks for the boys had been covered.

Amazing as it sounds, in the middle of the Ulster Championship, the Ulster All-Stars played two matches against Dungloe in Donegal on Wednesday evenings, which drew huge crowds.

On July 24th, Gallagher shot 0-7 in a draw that the local Democrat newspaper described as "the best exhibition of football seen in west Donegal in many years".

Frankie Kennedy, a member of the Ulster All-Stars, was by now a regular on the Cavan team at wing-back. That summer, he was working for the Department of Agriculture and was based in the east Donegal village of St Johnston, 15 minutes outside Derry. He and Charlie became close.

Gallagher would drive out to Kennedy's digs for a chat. At weekends, they would go to dances all over Donegal, to see the likes of The Clipper Carlton and the Royal Showbands.

When they returned to St Johnston, Frankie would walk in the front door and let Charlie in the window. His landlord later found out and wasn't pleased.

They often trained together on Gallagher's stomping ground, too.

"Charlie was a kind of a hero up there," Kennedy remembers.

"We used to train together in the Bogside. That was before it was called Celtic Park. Patsy Gormley that played with Derry and Sean O'Donnell from Donegal would be there, too."

Before the Ulster final, the training intensified. Gallagher had his own unique approach.

"I would run around the field; Charlie wouldn't. Charlie said that he would only do sprints. I said 'Charlie, that's not going to work, you'll have to do some long runs around the field'. Because this was beat into me in UCD.

"'No,' says Charlie, 'I'll do sprints.' I asked him why. 'I'll tell you why,' said Charlie, 'if I don't get the ball in the first five yards, I won't get it. But I f**king will get it.'

"And he would get it. When Charlie went for a ball [Kennedy claps his hands] bang! Gone like a light. He was the best man to take off. And when he went for a ball, he was in the air. You couldn't hit him. If you hit Charlie, he went up, instead of down. He had the best balance of any footballer I ever saw. Ever. You couldn't knock him down.

"He could score equally proficiently off his left, or right, over his shoulder. Equally. And he might come and say to you: 'What did you think of that, Frankie?'"

¶ ¶ ¶ ¶

Down were red-hot favourites for the final, having lost just one match in Ulster — the 1962 final to Cavan — in the previous five seasons.

Remarkably, the final was due to be reffed by Liam Maguire, a Garda based in Monaghan, who had actually won an All-Ireland medal with Cavan 12 years earlier. As it transpired, Maguire cried off due to a family bereavement and his place was taken by Jackie Martin from Tyrone.

Few believed the change of official would make a difference in any case. Down were fancied and only the most optimistic of Breffni followers gave them a chance.

¶ ¶ ¶ ¶

With 47 minutes gone in Casement Park, Cavan were running in treacle, trailing Down by 1-8 to 0-6. Joe Lennon had opened the scoring for Down with a spectacular goal after five minutes and only four frees from Gallagher kept Cavan in the game, as they trailed by 1-5 to 0-4 at half-time.

Despite two more frees from Gallagher, Down extended their lead and seemed set to win comfortably. Enter then 20-year-old Peter Pritchard as a sub for Cavan.

A point from Gallagher — now switched to full-forward — brought Cavan within six and then Pritchard struck, blasting a half-chance to the net. Suddenly, it was game on.

Another Gallagher free cut the gap to two and then came the defining moment.

"We were two points behind and Down got a 50 and Joe Lennon was going to take it," remembers Kennedy.

"Tom Maguire said 'I'm not going for this ball, Frankie, you cover me'. I was playing on Paddy Doherty.

"Anyway, Lennon kicked the ball in towards Tom's position and it screwed out to me and I got it. I kicked it down the field and Charlie got it around the middle of the field down along the wing and he kicked a big high ball in and Peter Pritchard stuck it in the net again."

Maguire had ignored the ball and had barged into Dan McCartan, the ref had missed it and Gallagher was in the right place to tear up the wing and square for Pritchard to do the rest.

"By now," wrote Peadar O'Brien, "the Cavan crowd were almost hysterical."

And their team weren't done yet. Thirty seconds later, Jimmy O'Donnell fired over a point and now, impossibly, they led by two with 10 minutes on the clock. The smash-and-grab was almost complete.

Down, like the champions they were, threw everything at Cavan in the closing minutes. The hits grew harder, the collisions wince-inducing. Cavan had dominated midfield, where Ray Carolan was immense alongside Tom Lynch, but Lynch finished the game on the sideline and the pressure piled on, with only Down goalkeeper Patsy McAlinden in their own half of the field.

"They were a hard, tough team," says Lynch, "but there were never any rows or anything like that. I know I had to go off near the end in Casement; Sean O'Neill hit me a fair shoulder, I didn't see him coming... I was seeing stars. I wanted to stay on but I had to go off."

Cavan managed one breakaway, Gallagher swinging over his eighth point on the counter but there was time for a final twist.

With time almost up, Down were awarded a free 21 yards out, and with their typical audacity, pulled a move straight from their playbook. Cavan lined the goals and O'Neill, always innovative, shaped up to take it. At the last second, he jumped over the ball and Doherty sent a rocket to towards goal but it struck the woodwork and went over.

Moments later, the final whistle sounded. Cavan had done the unthinkable again.

In previewing the game for the *Independent*, John D Hickey had tipped Down to win, throwing a few barbs the way of Cavan. Jim McDonnell had slowed down, he reckoned, and Tom Lynch's kicking was wayward. Most of all, Cavan's marksmanship up front was too shoddy, he posited, for them to win.

The game over, TP O'Reilly wanted his pound of flesh.

"It was a hot day and TP took off his shirt and he had a t-shirt underneath," says Lynch.

"JD Hickey was writing for the *Independent* at the time and he was above in the press box in the stand. TP had the cup and he was shaking it and saying, 'come down, Hickey! And he was the chairman of the county board!"

The Anglo-Celt Cup had been retired two years earlier; this time, McDonnell, as captain, was presented with the magnificent new cup, which still remains to this day.

Cavan were exultant but, after the match, when the madness died down, they made their way home as usual.

"Times were tough that time. After the final, we got ham and tomatoes in Belfast," says Kennedy.

"I was ravenous. Charlie says to me, 'Frankie, we can't go home. We'll have to celebrate winning the Ulster final'.

The North was a lonely place that time and we didn't want to hang around there on a Sunday, so we got our ham and tomatoes and we got back to Donegal. We got to St Johnston and Charlie says to me, 'We'll go to Cootehill!'. He had a posse of fellas in the car with him.

"So off we went and we arrived in Cootehill [80 miles

away] about 10 o'clock. And into the pub and of course, Charlie was the hero. I wasn't drinking, sure I was a student.

"And about three o'clock in the morning he put me in to drive the car and he had the others in cahoots with him. I drove it back to Derry and we were stopped by the RUC a couple of times. I dropped them all off and by the time I got to St Johnston, I could count the sheep on the hill — it was daylight.

"I went to work that morning at 10 o'clock, no sleep at all. Charlie would have been the same."

¶ ¶ ¶ ¶

The pressmen could not believe it. Somehow, Cavan had summoned another upset for the ages.

"The big weakness on the Cavan team on Sunday was its bad finishing and the scoring burst that brought victory only served to emphasise the debt that was owed to Charlie Gallagher, whose place-kicking had kept Cavan in touch with Down when everybody else was wasting opportunities," commented the *Ulster Herald*.

On the Sunday after the Ulster final, both Gallagher brothers lined out for Cootehill in a Senior Championship win over Virginia, splitting 14 points between them — six of Charlie's coming from play.

In the next round, the quarter-final, Charlie struck 1-6 including the winning goal as the Celtics dethroned champions Mullahoran.

The mid-week challenge games continued, too. Two days after the Mullahoran game, Gallagher lined out in an inter-firms match as a guest player for Du Pont Limited, a factory in Derry, against a Monaghan County Council side in Irvinestown.

By then, Cavan had gone into collective training for the semi-final against Kerry, starting in Kilnacrott on the first week of August. Aside from Tom Lynch — who was in New York on a holiday he had booked the previous April — and Gallagher, who joined in on weekends, there was a full turn-out and the mood was buoyant.

A church-gate collection was taken up one Sunday to cover the cost.

"I took two weeks off work and went down to Kilnacrott for full-time training. I was in the guards and I took time off without pay," says Morris.

"At that time in the guards, if you were playing football, they'd look after you. Kilnacrott was a boarding school that time and the students were gone off for the summer."

The players rose early each morning, walked the roads and trained under the supervision of Higgins, McDonnell and Matt Lynch. The craic was good and the panel had been strengthened by the addition of Phil Murray, Brian Morris and Joe Flaherty, while Anthony Dalton had been drafted in for the Ulster final.

They were quite a cast of characters and Dalton — who would end up coming on as a sub against Kerry — was extraordinary. In match reports, he was referred to as "P Nulty" (the quotation marks were included) because, as a seminary student, he was not supposed to be playing ball.

But he was too good to ignore. Born in Dublin, he came to Cavan after the death of his mother and lived with his aunt in Ballymachugh.

Aged 23, the future priest was an attacking half-back and one cool cat; cooler maybe even than Charlie.

"He was like Jesus, young, good-looking, tanned, had long hair and dressed like a cool guy. He drove an MGB GT. He set up a youth club in Ballymachugh called 'Amen Corner', because it was in the corner of the graveyard," remembers clubmate Peadar Gill.

By the time the All-Ireland final came around, Fr Tony had been ordained into the Oblate Fathers and was posted to Johannesburg. Two years later, after breaking his foot playing soccer, he decided to pursue his interests in horse-racing and shooting as he recuperated. True to form, he excelled and in 1968, he was chosen to represent Ireland in the Olympics but could not compete due to his missionary duties. However, he later won gold in the 4000m and Modern Pentathlon in the 1969 African Games, competing for South Africa.

He would later form a rock band, present a television show and study in Berkeley and Syracuse. His death, in a hang gliding accident aged 44, made front page news in his adopted country.

But that was all in the future. Here and now, the best footballers county Cavan could muster were ensconced in the old abbey and, leaving for Croke Park, they were certain of victory.

¶ ¶ ¶ ¶

In the build-up to the match, the *Celt* sportsdesk was inundated with nostalgic missives. In the pre-internet days, the paper was the forum where bets were settled. One correspondent wanted to know if it was true that Cavan had never beaten Kerry in Croke Park (it was) while another, the aptly-named 'Three More Pints' from Cootehill, enquired as to the starting teams from the final against the same opponents in the Polo Grounds 17 years earlier.

Another, W Kenny from London, got in touch with a leftfield suggestion that Cavan should include Brian Gallagher in the team for the Kerry game, reckoning "the two Gallaghers would score many points".

O'Neill, in his usual dry way, shut him down, replying that he didn't suppose the good doctor was "in the least bit interested in making a return to the Cavan team".

Several leading figures were canvassed for their opinions and none tipped the Ulster champions.

"Cavan, you know, were very lucky to get out of Ulster this year. If Charlie Gallagher is closely marked, I don't see how they could win," said Donegal's Mick Griffin.

Derry's Jim McKeever felt Cavan were "there with a chance" and that much depended on Carolan at midfield.

On the eve of the match, the *Celt* happily reported that the 20-year-old, who had been injured and taking it easy in camp, would be fit to play after all. Were he on form, the supply to the attack was guaranteed to be potent but that forward line, misfiring as a unit all year, remained an enigma.

"Come four o'clock on Sunday afternoon and before 50,000 on-the-spot onlookers and many thousands more watching on television, the hour of decision will have arrived for six men in the blue and white of Cavan," began Mick Dunne's preview.

"Their names — O'Reilly, O'Donnell, Pritchard, Cahill, Gallagher and McDonnell. On the shoulders of these six forwards rest Cavan's hopes."

Centre-back Tom Maguire was in no doubt, though, as to the key.

"Down played very well against us in the first half of the Ulster final but we wore them down," he said.

"Switching Charlie to full-forward was the winning of that game for us and I hope he is there on Sunday."

By the time the ball was thrown in, he was. And that was where the good news ended.

¶ ¶ ¶ ¶

Within 10 seconds of the throw-in, Gallagher had raced on to the ball and boomed over a point from 45 yards. And then, Cavan collapsed.

Kerry hit the crossbar before Tom Long goaled. The Kingdom's tackling was ferocious. By half-time, having played against a stiff breeze, they were ahead by 1-5 to 0-4 and, in the second half, they piled on the misery, running out 2-12 to 1-6 winners. For Cavan, it was an embarrassment.

Niall Sheehy blotted Gallagher out, the rest of the Cavan attack faltered and Long, Mick O'Dwyer and Bernie O'Callaghan were rampant up front. At midfield, Tom Lynch was taken off and Carolan should never have been playing in the first place. The selectors gambled on the youngster, the pulse of the side, and it backfired.

"I was lined out at midfield and the first time I had put a boot on me was on the Thursday before the match," says Carolan.

"I was playing on Mick O'Connell and the most humiliating thing ever happened to me. I was going over to pick a ball up along the Hogan Stand and I missed the first pick-up. Then I missed the second pick-up and Mick O'Connell came over and gave me a little push. I fell over and he picked up the ball and away up the field with it. That's as fit as I was."

By half-time, Cavan had used their three subs but it made no difference. The *Celt*'s post mortem was clinical and sharp as a surgeon's knife.

"Not since Kerry toyed with Monaghan in the 1930 All-Ireland semi-final has there been a sadder day for Ulster football. There has never been a worse one for Cavan."

TWELVE

Derry

The rain was lashing on the Lone Moor Road but that was not going to deter them; there was a bet to be settled. Out on the boggy surface of Celtic Park, home of Gaelic games in the soccer-dominated town of Derry; three friends were laughing in the wet and muck, kicking a rugby ball, determined to prove their own points.

Sean Moynihan was a Kerryman who taught geography in St Columb's College. Fr Ignatius McQuillan was a colleague from Fermanagh, a football man through and through. And with them was Charlie Gallagher, the highest scorer in the country.

Moynihan had worked for a time in Africa, where he had played some rugby, and reckoned that place-kicking with the oval ball required a mastery which Gaelic football did not. The others disagreed and it was decided that there was only one way to solve it, so off they went that afternoon.

"At that time, a lot of the kickers in rugby were really terribly bad. The ball could go anywhere," recalls McQuillan, now a monsignor.

"Charlie and me had an argument with Moynihan about which were the better kickers, the Gaelic boys or the rugby players. So we ended up later in the day, and it was a very wet day, going out to Celtic Park, which was an awful field at the time.

"We had a rugby ball and we had a kicking competition. And Charlie and me, we could kick them a lot better than Moynihan and he was a rugby player."

Then again, McQuillan and Gallagher had plenty of practice. They had met through Cully and soon struck up a friendship. Like the athletes they were, there was a competitive edge, too.

"We had a wee field — it used to be known as 'the college field' — and we used to go out there, Charlie and me, and have a kicking competition among ourselves.

"We would take it in turns placing the ball, wherever we wanted, and we would both kick frees from that same spot. In the end, we got quite good at it, we were scoring from all sorts of angles.

"Charlie was the leading scorer in the country for two years around that time and I think that had a lot to do with the practising we did out there."

¶ ¶ ¶ ¶

The 1947 Education Act had made secondary education free for any student who passed the Eleven Plus exam; suddenly, working class children, particularly from the Nationalist community, had a chance to make something of themselves.

In St Columb's, numbers exploded — by the mid-1960s, there were over 900 boys enrolled, triple what their had been during the war — and the teaching staff became young and vibrant.

With that came an extraordinary flowering of talent. Two Nobel Laureates, Seamus Heaney and John Hume; musicians Phil Coulter and Paul Brady; award-winning writers

Seamus Deane and Brian Friel; Irish Ambassador to Australia (among other nations) James Sharkey and political activist Eamonn McCann all attended St Columb's in the couple of decades that followed the passing of the Act.

It led to a time of awakening in the city, with the civil rights movement beginning to take flight in the mid-1960s.

"People with merit, with intelligence, were given the scholarship, so that talent brought forward a whole new set of people," Heaney would recall in the 2010 documentary The Boys of St Columb's.

"That arrival into the adult population, eventually, of educated people from the working class, from farming backgrounds, brought a new kind of critical intelligence, a new kind of appetite for excellence into play. They had a sense of adventure, a sense of themselves as a generation with some sense of possibility and advantage and renewal," he said.

That sense of adventure was present in 'Father Iggy', who had won an All-Ireland junior medal with Fermanagh in 1959 and was determined to raise the Gaelic football standards in St Columb's, which stood in the shadow of Celtic Park and also, Derry City's Brandywell grounds.

There was no question as to where the allegiances of the locals lay. Derry was a soccer town, through and through but Moynihan, McQuillan and others got to work.

They began with the younger age groups and worked their way up. In 1963, they won the McLarnon Cup, the 'B' competition at senior level.

The following year, they entered the prestigious MacRory Cup — the final of which Charlie Gallagher had played in nine years earlier, when the referee dropped dead — for the first time and reached the semi-final.

By '65, Fr McQuillan felt he had assembled a team which was good enough to win it. He roped in Gallagher as a mentor; training with the players an odd time, driving them to matches and they took it from there.

"He used to always help us with transport because schools that time had no buses or anything like that the way they have now. He would drive a few of the players and he enjoyed it.

"And it was great for the players to associate with him. He was a big name. It was a big thing for players at the time."

And so it must have been. The week after the 1965 MacRory Cup final, Gallagher picked up his first All-Star award and was named at full-forward in the fledgling 'Cuchulainn' awards scheme, under the auspices of the Gaelic Weekly GAA magazine.

St Columb's won that game by 1-13 to 0-4 against St Michael's of Enniskillen and in the ensuing Hogan Cup semi-final, stunned the aristocrats of the colleges game, St Jarlath's of Tuam, to reach their first final.

The final, against Dublin's Belcamp College, was fixed for Breffni Park and, it was reckoned in the papers, the presence of Gallagher in the St Columb's backroom team was certain to win over whatever neutrals from Cavan that were in the crowd.

Gallagher, who drove some of the St Columb's players to the game, had more pressing matters beforehand — the curtain-raiser of Cavan and Derry in the McKenna Cup.

Lining out at full-forward, he scored 1-4 in a 1-9 to 1-4 win before taking his place in the stand for the main event, which finished in a draw.

In the replay in Ballybay, though, history was made when the Derry lads ran out winners by a point, bringing a first-ever All-Ireland title to the county.

¶ ¶ ¶ ¶

Autumn, winter, spring. Same old, same old. In early September, Cootehill took to the field for the county final against Bailieborough. Gallagher hammered in an early goal and at half-time, there were two points in it but when Charlie went off injured early in the second half, the wheels came off and the Shamrocks ran away with it.

Two weeks later, Cavan played Dublin in a tournament game in Rush, losing by four, with Gallagher scoring 1-7. He followed that up with 1-6 in the opening round of the National League against Westmeath in Mullingar.

But Cavan slumped to a hiding at the hands of Galway in the semi-final of the Grounds tournament in Croke Park where Gallagher put up 0-7 in a 3-10 to 0-9 trouncing.

A week later, he bagged another 1-6 in a league win over Longford ("Charlie Gallagher was the star of the side and without him, the Cavan attack would be easily handled," surmised The Longford Leader).

Another six points followed in a narrow win over Leitrim, after which a letter appeared in the *Herald*, signed by a 'PH'.

"Sir," it began, "I would be pleased if you published a little tribute to Ireland's top scorer, Charlie Gallagher."

The poem, in five stanzas, sung the praises of the Cavanman.

"If I had money, time and tools/ A monument I'd build/ I'd paint it bright in blue and white/ And place it in Cootehill.

"I'd count the points that Charlie got/ On bronze I'd place them all/ And stand it high in his home town/ When first he played a ball."

The counting of points was done by *The Sunday Independent*, who published a weekly top scorers list. By the end of 1964, Gallagher was top of the pile with 6-103 in 19 games. On New Year's Eve in the same paper, JD Hickey reviewed the season and chose his top 10 footballers of the year. Galway, the All-Ireland champions, had the top three positions. In at four was Gallagher.

He picked up where he left off in the New Year. Eight points in a challenge against Louth, 1-4 against Meath and 0-7 against Mayo in Castlebar.

In early March, 1965, Gallagher — along with Kelly — was awarded his Cuchulainn award, the All-Stars forerunner, chosen by the GAA press. Two weeks later, he lined out with Ulster on St Patrick's Day, winning a second Railway Cup medal against Connacht on a day when Paddy Doherty scored 0-12, alongside Kelly, Morris, Carolan and captain Tom Maguire.

Gallagher was on fire by now. He landed 1-4 in a McKenna Cup game against Derry on the undercard to the Hogan Cup final involving St Columb's, adding 0-5 in the next round against Armagh and 1-10 in the semi-final against Monaghan.

¶ ¶ ¶ ¶

Seamus Hoare, who had played in goals in the Railway Cup win, was one of Donegal's most experienced players. A teetotaller, for Hoare the game was everything and came first to everything.

He was friendly with Gallagher, sometimes lining out in his All-Star games, but on the pitch, it was strictly business.

"Boys like Charlie don't come around too often. I often think he would have been a TV star nowadays. He had that charisma, he attracted people. When he came into the dance hall in Jackson's in Ballybofey, there was a buzz. 'There's Charlie Gallagher!'" Hoare recalls.

But there was a line he would not cross.

"When Charlie went for a drink, I would withdraw from him. I never drank, or smoked. My total emphasis was sport, I was dedicated to it. I could see the trouble with drinking.

"I liked Charlie but on the football pitch, of course I regarded him as the enemy. We had to stop him and there was only one way you could stop him, by being physical. You couldn't stop him by playing football.

"Because Charlie was two people. He was either brilliant or useless and he could stop playing, he would become a normal man. He wouldn't lead by example. Ray Carolan would be a different story — but he had different abilities. And you must have a mixture.

"Charlie was a bright star but he could be dimmed an odd time."

In the first round of the championship, Hoare's Donegal hosted Cavan in MacCumhaill Park. Donegal were six up at half-time, having struck 12 wides, but Cavan reined them in. In the last minute, they were a point down when Gallagher — who had, as usual, scored the opening point — clipped in a free via the upright. Draw game.

For the replay in Breffni, Hoare was plotting. The dressing-rooms were old, primitive Nissen huts and the walls were thin. He sidled up to Cavan's and put his ear to the wall to pick up whatever edge he could.

"I could hear the Cavan team talk," he smiles. "And it was very simple. The backs were to stay tight and the main instruction to everyone was to get the ball to Charlie as quickly as they could."

Even armed with this information, though, they couldn't handle him. Gallagher picked a defender's pocket and pointed the opener from 50 yards. Carrying a knee injury he had sustained on club duty against Kingscourt, he still managed 1-7 in a 1-11 to 0-14 draw. The tension in the closing stages was almost unbearable. For one follower, it was too much.

"As Breffni Park erupted in excitement that it was going to be a grandstand finish," reported the Donegal News, "few, except those near him, were aware that the stretcher men were removing the body of a spectator who had died around that time."

The teams retreated to the dressing-rooms to regroup after the full-time whistle. Cavan re-appeared but there was no sign of Donegal, who refused to play extra time. After half an hour, the ref called a halt.

Under rule, Donegal should have been thrown out but the Ulster Council didn't want to miss out on a "four-figure" gate, so two days later, at a special meeting, they fixed the third game for Breffni Park again, where the final instalment of the trilogy would be just as close.

Before the game, Hoare had instructed his corner-back on how to mark Gallagher. This time, there were to be no mistakes and the defender was to keep Gallagher shepherded to the wing and on his left foot.

Early in the game, Charlie grabbed possession on the

right wing and looked to cut in. The back, Dan McMenamin, did his job and forced him wide. Gallagher tried to sell a dummy but McMenamin wasn't buying so he turned back again.

At the third time of asking, Gallagher jinked and the defender pushed him onto his left foot, in the right corner. Charlie left fly and as the ball sailed over the black spot, McMenamin gave Hoare a look, as much to say: 'What can I do?' Hoare raised his palms skywards, shrugged his shoulders and got on with kicking out the ball.

Cavan versus Donegal matches in those years were fiery, known for their physicality. There was some bad blood and scores to be settled.

"In the second drawn match, I was playing wing-half-forward. After 10 minutes they put a different fella on to me and he said to me: 'I'm here to do a job on you, ya little effer ya. I'll sort you'," remembers Phil Murray.

"I didn't pass any remarks. But anyway a couple of minutes later he hit me a box and put me down. I got up and ran after him to hit him back and — now, he was a big fella — he hit me another box and put me down. And down I went like a ton of bricks.

"I got up again and got a couple of kicks at him but John Joe O'Reilly was on the forty and came down. Now, John Joe was a good guardian on the pitch for small fellas like me. And he comes running over and he shouts yer man's name.

"And as he turns round, John Joe hit him a box. And all I could see was blood flying. So at half-time Mick Higgins called me over in the dressing-room and he said: 'Do not get involved, they are trying to put you off your game, stay away from him'.

"But yer man came out in the second half and shook my hand and said: 'That's it, there will be no more fighting, look what happened me.' And he smiled, and he was missing his front row of teeth."

As the clock ticked down, Donegal thought they had done enough. They were two up with a few minutes to play when Gallagher pulled one back. With less than 60 seconds on the clock, he then converted a free to draw it and, with almost the final kick, substitute Seamus McMahon held his nerve to fire in a glorious winner, 0-9 to 0-8.

The newspapers sang the praises of the Cavan star, who had contributed seven of his team's nine scores.

"Charlie Gallagher was once again the Man of the Match for through his scoring and prompting, he kept Cavan in the hunt when they seemed ready to crack up," read the Donegal Democrat.

"As often before, Cavan can thank Charlie Gallagher for reviving their fortunes at a critical stage, for the Cootehillman worked feverishly in the last minutes when the chips were really down, darting from wing to wing to gain possession and endeavouring to land the much-needed scores," chimed the *Celt*.

In the semi-final, Cavan eased to a 1-10 to 0-4 win over Armagh, Gallagher kicking another seven points, but their exertions caught up with them in the final against, inevitably, Down.

Despite playing the better football in the first half, Cavan trailed by 2-1 to 0-5 at half-time. Gallagher was well held by Joe Lennon. In the dying seconds, the Blues poured forward and when Gallagher's 14-yard free was handled on the ground, he slotted the resulting penalty.

But it was too little, too late. Down were Ulster champions again, 3-5 to 1-8.

¶ ¶ ¶ ¶

For Charlie Gallagher, life was great. Business was booming. Cavan may have lost their Ulster title but he was an All-Star playing the best football of his career and even the St Columb's team he had been mixing with were the finest in the land.

The craic was good, too. He mixed well and was on friendly terms with patients from all walks of life. He had a great relationship with Barney Cully, his boss from whom he would later take over.

"When you met Charlie, you lit up," says Barney's son John.

"He would go down for his break and there was a little workshop within the practice where there was a dental mechanic employed making false teeth and stuff like that. Charlie would take his break down there and have a cup of tea and have fun.

"My Dad was very intense about his work and he would stick his head in and Charlie would slag him, 'ah Barney, come on in here and relax a bit!'. They got on well.

"If my dad was giving Charlie a bit of a lecture about something, Charlie would be winking at me. He was just boyish. He was so likeable.

"As a young fella, I was no footballer but I used to go out with him when he was practising frees in the local park and he would give me his Ulster jersey. And then, on a Monday morning, you'd see the paper and then see the star himself. We'd be asking him what it was like and he would be telling us stories. 'Oh, I'm a mighty man!' He was a character."

On a whim, Gallagher had taken up basketball, just to keep fit in the off-season. Word reached the *Independent*, who reported that "Gallagher is now bang on form, thanks to training with the Derry club, Eire Óg, and basketball, which he plays with Kerryman Sean Moynihan."

Fr Iggy played, too, and remembers Gallagher's uncanny knack for finding the basket. They cobbled together a team — Moynihan, McQuillan among the mainstays — and took to the hardwood.

"Charlie had this knack of making friends with a lot of people. And one of those was this guy who really came from a strong unionist background and he was on our team as well," he says.

"Charlie had this gift, as soon as he got into the other half of the court, he didn't have a great style for it but he could throw the ball into the net from anywhere. He was a natural. He wasn't that tall or anything.

"On one occasion, we were playing a team from up around the Protestant cathedral and they had this boy, he was a Mormon and he was over there for some reason.

"He had been a college player in America and played at a very high standard. We were so impressed by him and his style of play. We thought we better curb our own style a bit, be as nice as we could [laughs].

"But it turned out that this boy was very annoyed afterwards at how we were fouling all the time. And we were on our best behaviour! In the end, we beat them well. Oh now, there was always good fun when Charlie was about."

And then, at the end of '65, things got even better when he met the woman who would become his wife.

Maureen O'Donnell was a PE teacher whose father owned a physiotherapy clinic in Strabane, 15 miles from Derry and right on the Donegal border. Maureen was beautiful, intelligent, warm — and had no interest whatsoever in the sport which consumed her future husband.

"He used to come in at half six every evening to get this hamstring sorted with my father," says Maureen.

"I was talking to him and I asked 'where are you from?' And when he said 'Cootehill', I said 'where's that?'!"

She may have had no idea who the famous Cavanman was at first but the pair quickly hit it off. Soon, Maureen had been introduced to the family and noted that Charlie was particularly close to his mother, stopping in Russell's Bakery in Strabane to buy her buns on his regular journeys home for training and matches.

In November, 1966, Eva Gallagher felt ill and her husband thought it best to bring her to the Mater Hospital to get checked out. A priest had come in to visit her when she bent down to retrieve some money from her handbag and, just like that, passed away.

Word was sent to Charlie, who was grief-stricken. In Strabane, Maureen was taking a keep-fit class and returned to her parents' house afterwards, oblivious.

"I came back home and my mother and father said 'we had Charlie here on his way home'. I asked why and they told me his mother had died. It was an awful shock and Charlie, that whole winter, was very quiet afterwards."

The death, of course, hit Bernie Gallagher hard too. His daughter, Charlie's sister Eva, who was named after her mother, believed that he never got over it and was broken-hearted for the rest of his days.

"Whenever we would come down to Cootehill to see the father after that, we wouldn't get a word out of him," says Maureen. "He was very, very withdrawn."

"Grandad never smiled after Granny died," says Charlie's niece, Nuala. "We had to have all the blinds in the house in Cootehill halfway down the windows from the day she died. He grieved every day and would cry in his room. It was so sad.

"The family fell apart when she died, she was the glue."

In Derry, for her youngest child, life just had to go on.

THIRTEEN

Right Team, Wrong Time

Cavan were soon back in action, their understrength side losing to Sligo in the Gaelic Weekly tournament, with the Yeats men having already reached Croke Park for the first time ever. Gallagher was razor sharp, scoring 1-5 — the goal coming from a 21-yard free curled into the top corner — and rattling the crossbar twice, as well as laying on a goal for Pat Tinnelly.

Cootehill were knocked out of the Cavan Senior Championship by Bailieborough but on October 3rd, Charlie was back in action with Cavan, scoring 0-10 in a challenge match win over Fermanagh at Breffni Park.

The following Sunday, he scored 0-6 in the first round of the league in a loss to Longford and followed up with 0-7 in a win over Leitrim, which saw the experienced John Nallen — a well-travelled bank official, who had formerly played with Mayo, Meath and Galway and a friend of Gallagher's since the New York trip in '64 — make his debut at full-forward.

Christmas 1965 came and went and the first game of the New Year was on January 16th, Charlie landing 1-10 in a challenge win over Louth and and a week later, 0-7 in another friendly against Meath.

It went on. On February 6th, he scored 0-6 as Cavan gained revenge on Sligo in a league game postponed from earlier in the winter, with the team's new target man, 34-year-old Nallen, landing two goals. The *Celt* reported that Gallagher was in "his usual, ebullient form".

That win sent Cavan into the National League semi-final against Kerry in Croke Park. With Tom Lynch outstanding at midfield; Gallagher scoring 0-5 and teeing up Cormac Cahill for a goal. Cavan tore up the script with a five-point win.

"Unfancied Cavan scored a sensational victory over last year's All-Ireland finalists," reported *The Press*, with "Gallagher, in particular, extremely dangerous".

The *Independent* went further, awarding him their 'Sports Star of the Week' for his "cleverness and general accuracy". It was proof, not that it were needed, that Gallagher was now a household name, the top scorer in the country in the two preceding years and, having just turned 28, he was in his prime, playing the best football of his career.

Even in Kerry, where football folk are not easily impressed, Gallagher's name rang out, especially after that match in Croke Park.

Donie O'Sullivan, who played corner-back that day, still recalls, that by '66, Gallagher — yet to play in an All-Ireland final — was very much a national figure.

"Before I ever saw him playing, I had heard his name and heard about his magic from Michael O'Hehir on the radio. There was a buzz of excitement when Charlie got the ball," says former Kerry captain O'Sullivan, who would win four All-Ireland senior medals with the Kingdom.

"He would have been well-known in Kerry. He was a special player, so accurate. He was a scoring machine when things were going right for him but there was more to it than that, there was something about him. He was always togged out immaculately. I can picture him still with the black hair combed back.

"The first time I played against him was in one of those Wembley games [in 1963], he scored seven, or eight, points that day. He was so good.

"He had such skill, kicking-ability and speed, and there was something about him. I wouldn't say a strut but an air of confidence. Glamour, you could call it."

¶ ¶ ¶ ¶

Disappointment would follow on March 6th when Cavan lost the league final to Longford, 0-11 to 0-7, but on St Patrick's Day, Gallagher helped create some history when, despite the close attentions of his marker, O'Sullivan. Gallagher picked up a third and successive Railway Cup medal, as Ulster swept past Munster at Croke Park, with Carolan and Morris also on board.

The scores just kept on coming — 1-4 in a McKenna Cup draw with Derry and 1-3 in the next round against Armagh, which Cavan lost.

And then, on May 15th, probably Gallagher's greatest game: that 2-10 haul against Down in Carrickmacross which secured Cavan's trip to Wembley again.

An early switch freed him up and he caught fire.

"I was playing corner-forward and Charlie was left half-forward and Joe Lennon was marking him," says Phil 'Lightning' Murray.

"After 10 minutes, Charlie came to me and said: 'Lightning, you go out there and bring that fella on a run around the field. He has my head annoyed, I can't go anywhere without him following me.'

"So I brought Joe Lennon away up the field and he followed me everywhere I went, I barely touched the ball but Charlie had the whole space. He went to town that day."

The first goal came from a flick from Nallen, who was a huge physical presence and was striking up a good partnership — on and off the pitch — with Gallagher. The second was a through ball over the top which saw him dart between Tom O'Hare and Joe Lennon and send a rocket past Patsy McAlinden to the net. The points? Five in each half.

His deed was the talk of the country. At home in Crosserlough, 16-year-old Gene Cusack was listening to the Sunday night results show on RTE radio. Three years later, Cusack would break into the Cavan full-forward line alongside Gallagher to devastating effect,

"It's amazing what sticks in your mind," says Cusack, who by his own admission is one of those individuals who does not have vivid memories of his football career.

"Sean Ó Ceallacháin, as always, was reading the sports results late that Sunday night. He said: 'Cavan 2-13, Down 2-10. Charlie Gallagher 2-10'. To think one man could get that... I couldn't believe it."

In Wembley, against Sligo, it was more of the same. As usual, Charlie opened the scoring. He would finish with 0-7 to his name and two goals from John Joe O'Reilly and one from Lightning Murray were vital as Cavan cruised over the line, 3-10 to 1-10.

The only surviving footage of Gallagher in action is from this match and was shot by Jimmy Scanlon, a jeweller from Cavan Town.

The grainy, three-minute recording is tantalising. Murray's brilliant goal; a deftly chipped close-range free-kick from Charlie; the streaker and then the men in suits chasing him... and then Charlie, shot from behind, climbing the steps to the Royal Box and receives the gigantic, gleaming cup; his smile and his vivid blue jersey lighting up the otherwise dimly-lit shot.

After the presentation, the players file through, one by one, to shake hands with the ambassador and then the shot cuts to Charlie strolling on to the pitch. Amid the back-claps from fans, he holds the cup in both hands, escorted by a policeman who directs him towards an area on the pitch, in front of the stand, for a photograph.

Charlie, on his own, runs his left hand through his hair as if preparing himself for something. Lightning enters from the right; Charlie says something and they seem to be smiling. Tony Morris, Danny Brady and then the others arrive. A posse of photographers line up like a shooting party. And then it fades out.

That night, in the team hotel, the craic was mighty; Charlie was large and in charge, pulling pins on grenades and watching them go off. The team were billeted in the Atlantic Hotel in Bayswater. Sharing a roof that night was the musician Joe Dolan and his band, The Drifters.

Now, there were two problems. Firstly, Nallen was not a Dolan fan — the opposite, in fact. And problem number two was that Charlie knew it.

"John Nallen hated Dolan!" laughs Tom Lynch.

"And Dolan walked into the bar and after a while, Charlie started messing and Nallen and Dolan had words. Charlie was in his element and he was egging them on.

"Anyway, when we got home [to Ireland], John collected his Beetle and was heading back to Mayo. "On his way down west, he picked up a couple of lassies who were thumbing a lift and a bit down the road, what did they see only a big poster of Joe Dolan, saying where he was playing that night and the two women got all excited.

"And John was sick of it at this stage pulled up the car and put them out!"

¶ ¶ ¶ ¶

June 19th. Championship time. For the first time, Charlie would captain Cavan in the summer as Donegal come to town again. When the Donegal starting team was named, it caused a stir when future All-Ireland-winning manager Brian McEniff was handed his debut and, especially, when Sean O'Donnell — Charlie's friend — was moved from his customary wing-back slot to the corner.

The pressmen were in agreement that the switch was made for one reason — to counteract the Cavan captain. In an article headed 'Gallagher the man to watch', Peadar O'Brien reckoned as much in the *Press* but was fairly sure Cavan had the wherewithal to advance.

O'Brien couldn't have been more wrong. While Gallagher was rampant at corner-forward, burning O'Donnell for 1-4, at the other end, Cavan leaked like a sieve. At half-time, Cavan led by 0-9 to 1-3 and tacked on two quick points on the resumption but when Donegal came roaring back, the Breffni defence crumbled.

Hugh Barney O'Donoghue, vastly experienced out the field but a novice full-back, had a mix-up with goalkeeper Matt McHugh, a surgeon, and the ball snuck into the corner of the net — Donegal then took a scalpel to the Cavan defence.

Mickey McLoone played the game of his life and Cavan

were humbled at Breffni Park, losing by 5-6 to 1-11. Cavan had never before conceded five goals in a championship match. Another season was over.

¶ ¶ ¶ ¶

The Ulster Championship was over but the matches continued, thick and fast. Cootehill beat Cornafean in the first round of the championship (they would eventually be knocked out by Crosserlough) and, the following mid-week, Charlie was back across the border in Inishowen, scoring 5-4 for an All-Star selection in a charity game in Moville.

In August, Charlie pulled together a team for a fund-raising event in Lifford, Co Donegal. There were eight sides of nine players entered — six local clubs plus 'Charlie's Gallagher's All-Stars' and 'Sean O'Donnell's All-Stars', with each winning player to receive a suit-length.

The place was jammed each night for the GAA version of a Harlem Globetrotters exhibition. True to form, both All-Star teams made the final. Who won is not recorded.

¶ ¶ ¶ ¶

By the end of October, Sligo's Mickey Kearins landed 0-8 in a league game against Leitrim, bringing his total to 3-83 for the calendar year and leapfrogging Gallagher (6-68). Remarkably, that was the first occasion in 1966 that the Cavanman — who had not played an inter-county match in four months, remember, while others advanced their totals — was bettered in the national top scorers' list.

With the National League throwing in, Cavan followers were sceptical about their team's chances but it soon became apparent that something was building. Pat Tinnelly had slotted in the previous year in defence and young, speedy forwards Micheál Greenan and Steve Duggan were beginning to emerge.

With the arrival of Crosserlough's Andy McCabe — a notoriously physical defender whose youth belied his old-school approach — things were suddenly looking up.

Gallagher scored 0-5 and Greenan the winning goal in the opening league match against Sligo, now managed by Jim McCabe — in whose Beetle Gallagher and his student comrades had sat in to Galway way back in December of '58.

But an injury in that game, along with his mother's sudden passing, saw him spend a few weeks on the sidelines. By year's end, Gallagher was 'only' third in the national scorers list.

¶ ¶ ¶ ¶

It was February before Charlie returned and he was fairly subdued in Cavan's league win against Louth; although he did lay on the winning goal for Greenan and was fit enough to come off the bench for Ulster in a one-point win over Leinster in the Railway Cup semi-final at the end of the month.

However, he would be an unused sub in the final, as Connacht ended the northern province's hopes of five-in-a-row by a single point.

On March 12th, Gallagher scored six points of Cavan's 1-6 in the Division Two league final against Meath in Croke

Park; TP O'Reilly's son Garrett getting the goal as Meath won by the minimum.

The years were rolling by and, for Charlie, they had come to be defined by football competitions. League, Railway Cup, McKenna Cup, Championship, summer carnival and charity games, club championship, league and go again...

In early April, he scored 2-3 in a 7-7 to 1-6 McKenna Cup win over Fermanagh.

By now, Mick Higgins was also managing Longford. In the modern game, it would be unthinkable but back then, Higgins took it on. It was typical of the man.

Higgins had been approached by Fr Phil McGee, brother of Eugene's, and Jimmy Flynn, who persuaded him to also train the Longford team. As a test run, Higgins, canny as ever, organised a training session in Pearse Park in Longford on a night when he had two dogs running at the local greyhound track. He left the mutts in the care of a friend and ambled over to the pitch, where he found "more officials than players and just one football".

An ultimatum was laid down. A week later, he brought the dogs back to the track and, this time, on reaching Pearse Park, things had improved.

"Most importantly, there was a full squad at training and six balls," he would recall. And the greyhounds? Both won, naturally.

So, Mick was double-jobbing and already, Longford were on the rise.

"Higgins was an innovative coach," says former *Celt* journalist Eamonn Gaffney, who covered the team in the late 1960s and for four decades afterwards.

"One of his most successful tactics was employing the

roving full-forward gambit, which he initiated. Charlie was employed in this role by Mick in order to draw out the opposing full-back and leave room for the space to be exploited. Mick wasn't afraid of trying something new."

On April 23rd, inevitably, Cavan and Longford met in a Wembley Tournament play-off at Croke Park. In the first half, Cavan stank the joint out, falling seven points behind. And in the dressing-room, Mick — normally so quietly-spoken and mild-mannered — let rip.

"He tore into us at half-time and, kind of, said 'people will be laughing at me', something like that," remembers Garrett O'Reilly.

"I remember we won the game through sheer willpower. I don't think we played an awful lot better."

The young full-forward's memory is accurate. Cavan didn't really improve but they refused to lose. With Lightning Murray outstanding and Gallagher chipping in with three points, Cavan ground it out and their manager's blushes were spared.

¶ ¶ ¶ ¶

Cavan's inconsistency continued. They lost to Donegal, 3-13 to 0-11, in the McKenna Cup semi-final but on May 7th, hammered Kerry by 2-17 to 2-8 in Breffni Park in the final qualifier for Wembley — Charlie landing 0-9, including 0-7 in the first half.

With Tom Maguire having retired, Carolan was now at centre-back, with Lynch and Jimmy O'Donnell, forming an effective new-look midfield partnership and Greenan, who scored 1-3 against Kerry, proving a huge addition at wing-forward.

On Whit weekend, Cavan were off to London again. On Saturday morning, Carolan arrived into Dublin Airport from New York, where he had been lining out in the John F Kennedy Memorial Games, and quickly hopped on the 10.30am flight to London.

Galway, the three-in-a-row All-Ireland winners, were hot favourites to win but once again, Cavan came alive in Wembley to topple the Tribesmen, who lined out in an unfamiliar all-white kit for television purposes.

"Unprecedented scenes marked the end of one of the best Wembley Tournament games seen at the mammoth London stadium," reported the *Herald*, "when Cavan, with a great point from Charlie Gallagher in the first minute of injury time, beat the All-Ireland champions Galway by 1-11 to 1-10.

"The crowd rushed on to the pitch to cheer the Cavan men who certainly turned in their best display for many a day in the broiling heat of Wembley."

Early on, Cavan opened a two-point lead through Murray and Gallagher before Galway landed six in a row.

Then Gallagher pulled back another and, just before half-time, "tore past Martin Newell to send a hard, low shot under the diving body of Frank McLoughlin".

On the home stretch, there was nothing between them but a magnificent point from Greenan levelled it and, in the dying seconds, Charlie, who finished with 1-4, took a pass from John Joe O'Reilly and blazed over the winner.

"It would be an understatement," reckoned the *Independent*, "to say that this was one of the shocks of the season." The paper later awarded Gallagher their Sports Star of the Week accolade for the third time.

A Cavan fan in Tipperary summed up the general feeling with a letter to the *Celt* sportsdesk the following week. "Are Cavan back?" he asked, "that's the talk of the country at the minute."

¶ ¶ ¶ ¶

On June 18th, Cavan travelled to Casement Park to play Antrim for the first time in the championship since Gallagher's debut 11 years earlier. Goals from Murray and Greenan and eight points from their captain helped the favourites to a four-point win, with Seamus Martin in the Indo in no doubt as to the key man.

"As in their Wembley triumph, Charlie was again Cavan's star," he wrote.

"He was superbly accurate from frees and had a hand in most of his side's scores. So much is this side based on Gallagher, however, that one wonders how well they would play without him."

Leaving the field at half-time, Cavan leading by 1-7 to 1-6, *Irish Press* reporter Peadar O'Brien strolled down to pitchside and, most unusually, asked Gallagher for a comment.

"This is not good enough," was all O'Brien — who described Gallagher and Carolan as 'unplayable' — reported the Cavan captain saying in the next morning's paper.

Gallagher should have added a goal from the penalty spot, too, being denied by a brilliant save from Antrim goalkeeper George Eagleson five minutes from time.

Going into the semi-final against Tyrone, Gallagher was the second-leading scorer in the country with 3-48 to his name since the turn of the year, slightly behind Dublin's Jimmy Keaveney and just ahead of Sean O'Connell of Derry, who was by now lining out with for the Ballerin club in that county.

He would add five more points to that total after a routine 1-13 to 3-3 win over Tyrone in the semi-final.

As usual, Charlie was busy before the final. On the Friday after the semi, he lined out in an All-Stars charity game in Louth alongside a host of Cavan players and steller names such as Keaveney and Mickey Whelan from Dublin; Lennon and O'Neill from Down and Brendan Barden of Longford.

The evening before, he played for Ballerin in a tournament in Aghyaran in Tyrone; two days afterwards, he lined out in a challenge match for Cavan against Roscommon in Breffni Park. And the day after that, he scored Ballerin's entire total of 1-8 in the final of that tournament against Ballinascreen, which ended in a draw.

Coming into the decider against Down, amazingly, it was generally held that the Cavan defence was the team's weak link — a total turnaround on earlier years. The emergence of speedsters Duggan and Greenan and the switching of John Joe O'Reilly — a majestic, left-footed passer of the ball — had transformed the Breffni attack and, unusually for this era, they went in as slight favourites.

And they knew it, too.

¶ ¶ ¶ ¶

The 1967 Ulster final was fixed for Clones, a venue Down — wary that Cavan had stunned them twice in Belfast — had pushed for in the committee room.

Before the match, the Cavan squad met up in the Farnham Arms Hotel in Cavan Town and made a pact. There was to be no mistake this time.

"Any time Down ever beat Cavan, they got two goals in the first 15 or 20 minutes. Before the Ulster final in Clones in '67, the six backs got together and vowed that wouldn't happen," remembers Carolan, who was marking youngster Colm McAlarney, with Gabriel Kelly picking up Sean O'Neill.

"I knew we couldn't get beaten, everybody was up for the match. Leaving the Farnham, if I had £1,000 in my pocket I'd have put it on Cavan to win. We got on the bus and it was so calm, it was unreal. There was so much confidence there.

"After about 20 minutes we had held them at bay and I remember going round to the boys and saying 'come on lads, we have them beat now'. And we destroyed them after."

Carolan can recall the ferocity of Cavan's play.

"James McCartan was coming through with the ball," he says, "Peter Pritchard came across and hit him a shoulder and, before he straightened up, Andy McCabe came across and hit him from the other side."

McAlarney was playing in his first Ulster final and recalls how fired up Cavan were.

"We were beaten, deservedly so, that day," he remembers.

"I was playing centre-half forward against the great Ray Carolan. Ray was centre-half back that day, although we would have had duels in midfield after that, but that day he had a stormer — he was one force of nature.

"We had huge respect for that Cavan team. It's funny,

Charlie Gallagher

Charlie Gallagher, whose general cleverness and accuracy—he scored five points—helped Cavan to score a shock win over Kerry in the National League, Division 2, semi-final at Croke Park last Sunday.

Charlie Gallagher

Charlie Gallagher, Cavan's sharp-shooter who, in scoring 2-10 against Down in last Sunday's Dr. McKenna Cup tie, had one of the best games of his career.

This Week's Personality

● Charlie Gallagher, the free-scoring Cavan corner forward, is this week's Sports Personality. In helping his county beat Down in the Wembley Tournament qualifying game at Carrickmacross on Sunday, Gallagher scored 2-10 of his side's 2-13 total. He is the unanimous choice of the Sports Desk.

Gallagher was regularly selected for accolades by the GAA press.

Winning one of his four Railway Cup medals with Ulster in 1966.

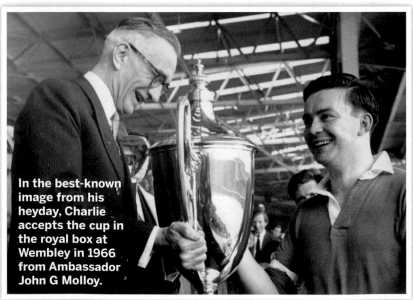

In the best-known image from his heyday, Charlie accepts the cup in the royal box at Wembley in 1966 from Ambassador John G Molloy.

The Cavan team whom Charlie (front, centre) captained to the Ulster title in 1967 pictured before and (below) after the win over Down.

Charlie captained what was, by common consent, the best Cavan team never to win an All-Ireland – they are pictured here before a one-point semi-final loss to Cork in 1967.

Charlie lining out in 1968.

Charlie and Maureen pictured on their wedding day in Strabane in 1968. Note the onlookers straining to see the couple! Right: A newspaper report on the 'wedding of the year'.

Strabane bride for captain of Cavan team

The bride and groom prior to the cake-cutting ceremony.

A view of Market St in Cootehill in 1969. The Gallagher home was on the left, a few doors up.

The Cootehill Celtic team which won the JFC in 1969.
Charlie is fifth from left, back row.

A formal note, hand-signed by chairman TP O'Reilly, informing Gallagher that he had been selected to represent Cavan in the 1969 Ulster SFC final in Casement Park.

cumann lúit-cleas gaedeal Coisde Úreirne Uí Ragallaig

Telephone: Cavan 304.

Woodford,
Ballyconnell,

CABHAN .... 22nd July, '69.

A CHARA,

You are selected to play with the Senior County Team versus
Down, ... at Belfast.
on Sunday 27th July.

Please bring Boots, Togs, etc. Travelling arrangements as follows: ~~XX XXX XXX~~
~~XXX XXX XXX XXX XXX XXXX~~ Make out your own travelling
arrangements, and be in Park at 3 p.m.

Mise do Chara,

NOTE— Any player failing to turn out without proper cause is liable to suspension
If from any cause a player is unable to play, the Secretary must be
notified as soon as possible.

The Cavan team which Charlie captained to beat All-Ireland champions Down in the 1969 Ulster final.

In action during the 1969 Ulster final against Down (left) and collecting the Anglo-Celt Cup after the victory (above).

Charlie (front, centre) with the Cavan team who drew with Offaly in the infamous 1969 All-Ireland semi-final.

Cootehill Celtic make a presentation to Charlie and Maureen in 1970 to mark Charlie's retirement from inter-county football.

Celebrating winning the 1973 Cavan Senior League with Sean Foy (centre) and John Joe Tierney, captain of Cootehill Celtic when Charlie made his debut in 1953.

Filling the cup in Tommy Connolly's bar in 1973.

Lining out for Cootehill Celtic c1973.

Charlie is honoured on the *Sunday Independent/* Irish Nationwide 'Greatest Team Never to Win an All-Ireland' in 1984.

Attending the Cavan GAA board convention as a Cootehill Celtic delegate in 1985.

Charlie's funeral cortege in Cootehill in July, 1989. PIC: IAN McCABE

Charlie's grandchildren Charlie, Rian, Finlay, Ellen, Emily and Connor, all of whom are keen GAA players.

Right: Charlie's grandchildren Connor, Charlie and Rian with three of their grandfather's jerseys at Hugh O'Reilly Park in Cootehill.

though, how you think you're right and you're not and it's too late when you find that out in the white heat of a Championship match.

"In those days, Cavan were coming, breathing fire, and unless you were ready to run through brick walls, you were going to be on the receiving end and we certainly were in '67."

By the time the full-time whistle sounded, Cavan had run out 2-12 to 0-8 winners; Greenan and John Joe O'Reilly again with the goals and Gallagher chipping in with six points.

Charlie received the Anglo-Celt Cup as captain for the first time. It was arguably his greatest day, an afternoon where he displayed his wondrous skills on the big stage.

For McAlarney, greater days lay ahead but he considered it a privilege, even in defeat, to share the field with the likes of Kelly, Carolan, Lynch, Murray and, of course, Gallagher.

"I was coming into my career and Charlie was coming towards the end but was still a formidable player and played very, very well against us.

"As a player I would describe him as almost a little bit portly — a little bit of weight but not much but that was deceptive because he was very quick off the mark. 'Sharp' is the word.

"That was an era when players tended to keep their positions but Charlie was very cute and leaving space for ball being delivered into, he was very sharp on that first ten yards.

"He was going to get there and when he would get it he had such silky skills that, for a defender, he was a nightmare because it was so difficult to take it off him and then he was very accurate. So, he had it all."

The newspapers had a field day. Cavan — so brilliant on their day, so unpredictable — made for good copy and so did Gallagher. Every national paper carried his image and word of Cavan's feat in finally and emphatically returning to the throne.

"Of all the many triumphs the blue-jerseyed repre-sentatives of Breffni have etched into the annals," wrote Mick Dunne, "few can have been sweeter than this, for it was achieved on the same pitch on which Cavan, in 1959 and 1960, lost their only Ulster finals to Down."

The report in the Examiner, under the heading 'Galla-gher stars for Cavan', was all about one man.

"I am not suggesting that this is a great Cavan team but they have a devilishly difficult individualist in 'Cheeky Charlie' and a flair for natural football against which there can be no preconceived answer... Unless Cork negate Gal-lagher, they could be in trouble."

The unnamed staff reporter was wrong, though. This was a great Cavan team, by common consent the greatest since the All-Ireland-winning sides. Since they last won Ulster, Andy McCabe, Pat Tinnelly and Brendan Murtagh had seamlessly slotted into the defence, in front of new goalkeeper Seamus Galligan with Brendan Donohoe assisting Lynch at midfield.

And up front, it was no longer a one-man show. John Joe 'on the 40', Duggan, Greenan and Lightning, along with Jimmy O'Donnell, were all high-class ball-players.

"Previously, we were expecting Gallagher to carry the whole show on his shoulders up front but now we have six oustanding forwards," said county vice-chairman Tommy Gilroy, a selector when Cavan lost the All-Ireland final to Cork 22 years earlier.

Now, it was again Cork who stood in their way in the All-Ireland semi-final where, surely, Cavan would finally put things right.

But information was sketchy. Tom Maguire admitted to Dunne that "none of us have seen Cork lately" while county secretary Hughie Smyth described the Munster champions as "an unknown quantity".

Higgins agreed ("We know nothing about Cork. I'd much prefer a team we know") and Paddy Donohoe, the county treasurer, summed up much of the reason for Cavan's confidence.

"The days of stopping one man and holding the Cavan forward line are gone," he said. "Our forwards are now firing on all six cylinders and the Ulster final proved it."

¶ ¶ ¶ ¶

When the Cavan players of the 1960s look back now, '67 is the one they rue. That Cavan squad had a rare balance of power and grace, experience and energy.

The attack was mobile and always on the move. Gallagher roved anyway but the addition of the young wing-forwards seemed to be the final piece in the jigsaw.

"Myself and Duggan probably started something," says Greenan, "we used to switch wings. The whole idea was would the wing-backs go with us or stay where they were. They were in two minds. It worked well."

Greenan believes that the 1967 team was the best of the era and most concur. They should have beaten Cork in the All-Ireland semi-final. That they didn't, losing by a point, is down to sheer bad luck.

"I've no doubt that '67 was really the year we should

have won it, there's no doubt about that. It was the best of the teams that time."

Somehow, Cavan managed to lose 2-7 to 0-12 to the Rebels. Steve Duggan, in common with his teammates, talks about two penalty decisions — one was given, one wasn't. Both calls, Cavan believed, were wrong.

"We reckoned that day we should have got a penalty that we never got. Cork got a penalty that they shouldn't have got. Someone pushed Peter Pritchard and he fell on the ball and they gave a penalty. It should've been a free out. Cork beat us."

Said Greenan: "As a former referee I hate to be critical, but Cavan felt he didn't do us many favours that day.

"For the first goal, Seamus Galligan and Pritchard collided and yer man put the ball into the empty net. The next one, someone caught a ball and fell with it in their hands and the ball hit the ground. Penalty. I actually felt it was a free out because he was fouled but that's what happened."

Garrett O'Reilly feels the same.

"There was a penalty we definitely should have got. We had a last-minute free to equalise it but we lost by a point.

"Mick Burke played midfield for Cork that day and he was brilliant. We were told don't worry about Burke; Mick O'Loughlin was the man to watch at midfield. But Burke had a storming game.

"We conceded two terribly soft goals. John Joe [O'Reilly] was pulled down on the square, it was clearly in the square but we got no penalty."

Carolan still regrets not speaking up and insisting he line out at midfield. It wasn't the done thing at the time and nobody was going to question Higgins anyway. But it was an error.

"I was centre-back and Mick Burke was playing midfield and he beat Cavan on his own that day. He dominated the game, had a field day.

"He played with Munster in the Railway Cup and I played him in two finals and he was one of those fellas I could always play the socks off. He came to me after the match and said: 'I couldn't believe they didn't put you in midfield'.

"We were unfortunate, too. We gave away a penalty — it was questionable.

"It was very negative thinking because my belief was that if I was playing in the middle of the field, we could get the ball up into the forward line. The management wanted to block off the back-line and not let other fellas score.

"We got caught because we didn't place the team right."

Years later, when asked what his greatest disappointment in football was, Charlie, who scored 0-8 of Cavan's total, didn't hesitate in nominating that 1967 semi-final.

"This was one game," he said, "that Cavan should have won."

To rub salt into the wound, Burke collided with Meath's Red Collier in the final and went off injured after 10 minutes. The Royals won and headed off on what Duggan described as "the best trip ever — to Australia".

There was a priest at the time, Fr Tully, the chairman of the Meath county board, who was famously anti-Cavan. He declared that Meath were not worthy All-Ireland champions until they had Cavan beaten.

So, when the Royals returned, Cavan played them in the Grounds Tournament final and won.

"We could beat everyone on a given day, we showed that time and again. But not just on the right day," says Greenan, shaking his head. "It was unreal."

The right team, the wrong time...

¶ ¶ ¶ ¶

The dust had barely settled on the crushing loss to Cork when rumours began to circulate that Charlie was considering packing it in.

A correspondent using the pseudonym 'True Blue', from Dundrum in Tipperary, got in touch with the *Celt* to confirm the chatter doing the rounds.

"I am anxious to know," he wrote, "is it true that Charlie Gallagher, Gabriel Kelly and Jimmy O'Donnell are thinking of calling it a day. This would be a big blow to the team.

"I think Charlie Gallagher's absence from the forward line would be a terrible blow to the present set up. Charlie is the greatest scoring forward Cavan has ever produced.

"His name, down here in Tipperary and the surrounding counties, is mentioned as often as John Doyle, Jimmy Doyle and Christy Ring — he is just a household name everywhere.

"I do hope," he concluded, "that he, Gabriel and Jimmy will give us at least one more year of their brilliance and that Charlie will receive the Sam Maguire Cup in 1968."

With 5-94, Gallagher had finished 1967 as the country's highest scorer again, 20 points clear of Dublin's Jimmy Keaveney in second — all this despite playing a handful of matches at the tail end of the year with a hamstring injury picked up in the Grounds Tournament final.

Cavan's form, as usual, was up and down. In February 1968, Gallagher scored 0-9 in a win over Derry and, on March 10th, the winning point in yet another filthy encounter with Donegal in a play-off in Carrick-on-Shannon.

"All that is worst in Gaelic football was shamefully in evidence as this match deteriorated into a tempestuous and vicious brawl," reported Mick Dunne, who described the match as "an appalling travesty of sport".

Cavan players still recall this one; there was often blood and thunder at Cavan versus Donegal games but that match still resonates in particular.

"Donegal and Cavan used to have it fairly rough at the time. There were several little shemozzles this day," recalls Tom Lynch.

"Two boys were at it anyway and Gabriel was in between them trying to split them apart. And I came up behind and threw a fist."

Kelly: "I saw a fist coming over my shoulder and whack yer man!"

Lynch: "Later on that evening, the two teams ended up in the one hotel and I was in the toilet and yer man comes in with a black eye. I said, 'Jaysus, what happened you?' He says, 'Some hoor hit me a belt!'

"'Did you not see him?' 'No,' he says, 'I didn't'. 'Jaysus,' I said, 'that's a terror...'"

Cavan won that one but they would crash out of the league at the hands of Sligo, with Charlie visiting the winners' dressing-room to congratulate them afterwards.

On St Patrick's Day, he picked up a fourth Railway Cup medal; the captain scoring 0-3 in a win over Leinster at Croke Park, having earlier beaten Connacht in the semi-final in Cavan. Winning the competition for the first time was a 19-year-old Colm McAlarney from Down, who partnered Ray Carolan at midfield.

"The Railway Cup was massive in that period," says McAlarney.

"Especially in the sixties, huge crowds attended and when I made my debut, Charlie was captain.

"That was a Railway Cup-winning team but looking back at pictures, it shows you where the power lay at that time with five or six players each from Cavan and Down and with two others each from Derry and Donegal. That's where the power lay in Ulster."

McAlarney was fast-emerging as one of the best young players in the country, having made his senior debut while still a minor. Yet coming into an Ulster dressing-room including the likes of Seán O'Neill, Seán O'Connell and Gallagher, he was nervous.

"I have a vivid memory of coming into that dressing-room in Breffni Park and the butterflies in my stomach and being warmly welcomed by Charlie.

"He put me at ease because here I was, a callow youth sharing a dressing-room with all these icons. So, those kind of touches were very important and something I learned from people like Charlie for later on in my career; for whenever young players came into a dressing room at county level, or provincial level, or whatever. You made sure to introduce yourself and make them feel welcome, so that was an important touch from Charlie. He was a very pleasant man, very good for banter and craic and things like that even though there was a great rivalry there, there was also respect and camaraderie.

"When those things linked together it was important because Ulster, at that time, won the majority of the Railway Cups, which was the only representative football out-side your county."

Cavan would eventually lose the deferred Grounds Tournament final, a qualifier for Wembley, to Mayo by 1-10 to 1-7; Gallagher notching 1-4, including a spectacular goal. But Charlie would get to London, either way. The only difference would be that instead of his teammates, he would be accompanied by his new bride.

¶ ¶ ¶ ¶

The wedding of Charles Oliver Gallagher and Maureen O'Donnell, in Maureen's home town of Strabane, took place on April 20th, 1968. The sun shone and the wedding party were sensational.

The *Strabane Chronicle* devoted half of its front page to the event, carrying two large photographs.

"Traffic was held up and the spacious Church of the Sacred Heart was unable to house the capacity congre-gation when the wedding of the year took place on Satur-day," they reported.

Maureen arrived with her father, Hugh, in a pony and trap and fully-attired coachman for the Mass, which was co-celebrated by Fr Iggy McQuillan.

The newspaper reports focused heavily on the style on show ("Leaving for the honeymoon in London, Mr Galla-gher favoured a three-piece of French design, with red and white accessories").

The photos show a beautiful couple, surrounded by family and with Maureen's students gawping in admira-tion. The reception took place at the Knock Na Moe Cas-tle Hotel in Omagh.

THE STORY OF CHARLIE GALLAGHER

"Charlie was on for inviting people from teams and it was going up into huge numbers — my father would have just seen red!" laughs Maureen.

"So, it was just nobody outside the families at all. Nuala was living in England, Brian was in England and Eva was in Wicklow. Angela was in Dublin, Leonora was in America, 'Leo' didn't make it home for the wedding.

"Of course," she added, "the cake had to be royal blue and the bridesmaids had to be royal blue."

Charlie insisted on that.

The football summer petered out with an injury-hit Cavan losing the Ulster final to Down, who, typically, went on to win a third All-Ireland. Off the field, things were changing fast. Soon, Charlie would be a family man, although, in ways, he always had been.

"My Dad died when I was 12," says Nuala Marcelin-Horne, his niece, "and Charlie became ours until his own family came along. Maureen was our favourite aunt and she was the love of his life. Their wedding was on the front page of every newspaper in Ireland and I still have a copy of the one in *The Press*. Always loved.

"He was the kindest person in my life. I have so many happy memories of staying with him in his digs in Derry when he was a young, fit footballer playing for Cavan and Ulster. I used to go with him to watch him running and training every evening. He was absolutely dedicated. When at a match, he would ask me to shout 'Come on, Cavan' and not 'Come on, Uncle Charlie'. That was his nature."

FOURTEEN

Say It A Bit Louder

Charlie's in the bar and the joint is hopping. *Danny Boy* is his favourite tune.

"Oh Danny Boy, the pipes, the pipes are calling." Charlie has always had a great voice and he loves to sing.

This is early summer, 1968, and there's not a big drinking culture around football teams. Ordinary punters just don't have the cash, for one thing. Not the players and not the supporters, either.

"There was no-one used to any money. Charlie, yeah, would have been used to a few pound but there were others who wouldn't have had the price of it," remembers Dessie O'Sullivan, a neighbour from outside Cootehill and a walking encyclopedia on the game.

"But you had the football and you had Charlie Gallagher, he was the man we all wanted to see."

Tonight, they all get to meet him, and three friends, too. The Anglo-Celt Cup, the Railway Cup and the O'Gorman Cup from Wembley were all in tow.

After a match, there isn't much drink taken. Charlie would have a few, John Nallen, maybe Jimmy O'Donnell and Matt McHugh but not many others. Most were teetotallers, pioneers.

The place is heaving. Dessie, a couple of years younger than Charlie, was there for all the big wins, or most of them anyway.

When the team won in Wembley, Dessie didn't make the match but he was in attendance for the after party, such as it was.

"I wasn't at the game. My brother got married up in Hayes and I was late back to the airport. I was panicking a bit but I wasn't five minutes there till I saw the Cavan bus and Charlie getting off it and then Jim Rice and Harry McMullen and Tommy Reilly, they had all come over from Cootehill to support the team.

"Charlie said to me, 'come on the flight with us back to Belfast'. I think I gave them an extra pound or so and I did that, Charlie had the car in Belfast."

On the way south, they stoppped in Monaghan, at the Westenra Hotel, for a drink. Charlie was in the prime of his life, soon to be married, possibly the most talented footballer in Ireland.

Pit stops. Pubs. If the game was in Cavan, it was the Farnham Hotel. In Cootehill, there was an assortment, with all roads leading, usually, to Tommy Connolly's. Around Croker, there was Barry Hotel, Fagan's in Drumcondra.

And on the road to Derry, Reilly's in Newtownbutler. Flood's in Pettigo, another place in Ederney. And then, on a jaunt out of the city and across the border, MacIver's in Burnfoot. Football houses. Not all at once, you understand, but in moderation. Charlie was a socialiser, someone who loved meeting people and having fun and was always ready with a memorable one-liner.

Peter Brady remembers a scene from a Sunday in Navan in the mid-60s on the way home from a Railway Cup final win in Croke Park. Gallagher was holding court in a pub full of Meathmen and one approached him.

"Your man says are 'you Charlie Gallagher?' and Charlie says 'I am'.

"'Jaysus I have to shake your hand', he said, 'you killed us in Pairc Tailteann in one game ya hoor ya, you scored a point from the left-hand line, 50 yards out in the first half and you did the same in the second. Do you remember it?'"

"'Oh I do', says Charlie, glancing around, 'but say it a bit louder!'."

Another happy customer.

Most places he went, people knew him, knew the smile, wanted to hang out with him and be able to tell their friends that they had, too.

"What I remember about Charlie," recalls Donal O'Grady, a teammate from 1962 to '66, "was he was the happiest, jolliest fellow you could meet on earth and he absolutely loved playing football."

"He was just great craic," says Steve Duggan.

"He was a great singer. I think he used to sing Old King Cole. And Charlie would make up his own lyrics as he went along. He was great fun and everybody respected him and I think absolutely everybody wanted to be in his company.

"I mean, there would be people swarming round him. Sure people loved him and wanted his autograph. He would talk to anyone, no big head about him, no big deal. He was just one of our own."

Maureen, though, would be mortified at the adulation. She hadn't been a football fan when they started going out and was amazed at how people reacted.

"The worst time, I think, was the year we were married, we went to Kerry and we were staying in a wee B&B

in Sneem and went to the Parknasilla for the evening meal. It was a beautiful, beautiful summer. He went up to the bar and I was sitting waiting and the next thing the fella behind the bar got all excited and says 'God, are you recognised everywhere you go?!'

"It echoed all over the place. These American tourists were all sitting round. They thought we were film stars or something! I'll never forget it."

Here in Cootehill in 1968, there are 24 pubs, all doing a trade. Business picks up when Charlie comes home.

"When he came home at weekends for a match, he would always stay over till the next Monday morning," says Foy.

"All the boys that would be hanging round the corner would be waiting for Charlie to go into a certain pub and they'd go in there then and Charlie would put a fiver up on the counter, 'Give the boys a drink'.

"He'd throw the fiver up and the change wouldn't come back. A fiver was fierce money that time, a bottle of stout would have been only a couple of shillings.

"He was very generous, good-natured. You had to be good-natured to be a dentist, anyway, everybody is tender and sore. But he was very kind-natured, he was."

Ordinary folk saw it as a privilege to press the flesh with Charlie Gallagher. They could be star-struck.

Duggan would break into the team as a teenager in '67 and would embrace the social side of things, too. After one match, he and Charlie ended up in Duggan's local, Donohoe's in Ballyhaise.

"Charlie stayed the night in my mother's house and he had to get up at six o'clock the next morning, he had an appointment at nine o'clock in Derry.

"So my mother got him up out of bed and made him his breakfast. Sure it was an honour to have him in the house.

"And my brother Mike happened to be home from England at the time and I will never forget, he was playing the accordion for Charlie at six o'clock in the morning as Charlie ate his breakfast."

A salute fit for royalty. And here in Cootehill, the king is on his throne, the cups are gleaming and cameras flashing.

Does he know it won't last forever? Can it ever? Charlie clears his throat and the hush descends. That old favourite, of his and theirs.

"And I'll be there, in sunshine or in shadow."

FIFTEEN

No-One Knows

Another season had breathed its last and soon, the footballers of Cavan, smarting from seeing Down waltz to a third All-Ireland in nine seasons, were back at it, turning the car for Breffni Park a couple of times a week.

Gallagher's form had deserted him. While he had scored 1-4 in the Ulster final the previous July, as part of a season's tally of 4-61 that left him fifth in the national scoring rankings, Charlie would soon turn 31 and there were signs of slippage.

His dalliance with Ballerin Sarsfields in Derry had ended and Cootehill's stock had plummeted. By the end of '68, Cootehill would successfully apply to be regraded to junior ranks, despite concerns from some clubs that, well, they still had Charlie and presumably, Charlie still had IT.

Yet there were indicators there that he had not — that he could still hear the music but his feet were no longer keeping time to the beat.

In late October, he made the short trek to Ballinascreen to play Derry in the opening National League match of the 1968/69 season. It ended in a draw; he didn't play well.

A couple of weeks later, in the league, Cavan beat Longford, managed by Mick Higgins, who had led Longford to their maiden Leinster title the previous summer. For the only time in his career, Gallagher was held scoreless.

It was literally headline news, unprecedented. After

that came the break for Christmas and when Cavan returned to action in the New Year, they did so without their regular Number 13, who, rumour had it, was toying with hanging up his boots.

The papers had picked up a sniff of the story and ran with it before a late-March National League play-off against Donegal in Dungannon; a dog of a match which erupted into chaotic scenes at the final whistle.

In the event, Gallagher did play, coming on as a sub in the first half and scoring 0-4. What led to the ruckus was that Donegal's late winner, in the opinion of the travelling players and fans, was wide.

"That's the hardest match I have had in seventeen years as a referee," was the reaction of Tyrone whistler Patsy Devlin immediately after a game, which Donegal won by 0-10 to 1-6 with two Cavan followers trying to make their feelings known to Devlin at full-time.

So, Gallagher was back and installed as captain again but doubts persisted. The following week, the delayed 1968 McKenna Cup final, against All-Ireland champions Down, was to be decided.

"If Charlie Gallagher is near peak-fitness, his mere presence around the square will cause panic," predicted the *Celt*.

On April 20th, Cavan beat Down by a point in the final in Ballybay but Charlie was far from his best. A photo-graph of him, as captain, receiving the cup, match ball under his arm, was proof that he had wintered well; his cherubic features told their own story.

Still, at least he was back in the fold — with him, there was always a chance, although there was an awareness there that time was running out.

"This is probably the last chance that such great players as Gabriel Kelly and Charlie Gallagher have of winning an All-Ireland medal," warned a letter-writer to the *Celt* that very week.

Seven days later, the shortest reign as McKenna Cup champions in history came to an end, when the 1969 competition threw in and Cavan were dumped out; Donegal — again — winning by the minimum, 1-10 to 1-9.

Optimism was low entering the championship. First up was Fermanagh, in Irvinestown, and memories were still fresh of how Gallagher's two lucky goals had helped scrape past Fr Iggy and Co at the same venue nine years earlier.

On this occasion, they were just as fortunate, holding on to win by 1-9 to 2-4, one report lashing them as "ill-prepared, ill-conceived and certainly ill-equipped".

After the match, county chairman TP O'Reilly let rip in the dressing-room. The hero of the Polo Grounds was known for it ("TP would get very excited but we all loved him because he was very enthusiastic," was Carolan's typically good-humoured summation) but this particular performance probably deserved it.

And yet, before the semi-final against red-hot favourites Derry, the Ballyconnell solicitor was more upbeat, referring to the close shave in Irvinestown as "the best thing that ever happened to us".

And it probably was. For 10 successive evenings after that game Cavan trained. Gallagher was getting sharper by the day and shedding the pounds. Midfielders Carolan and Hughie Newman were purring.

When the team was named, though, for the semi-final, Charlie was demoted to the bench. For the first time in his

Cavan career, it seemed he was no longer an automatic selection.

At corner-forward all Spring had been Crosserlough's Gene Cusack, an electrifying, powerful score-getter. At just 19, he was already developing into Cavan's go-to man. Far from begrudging him, though, Gallagher went out of his way to help Cusack — who, it was clear, would soon be vying for the same starting position — settle into the set-up.

"I wouldn't have a great memory for football but certain things stand out. I always remember when I came in to the Cavan senior panel, how welcoming he was," says Cusack.

"I don't know what match we were going out for but I clearly remember him saying to me 'you're the best piece of work ever I saw, you go out there and teach them a lesson'.

"I thought to myself at the time — he was number thirteen — I was after his jersey and yet this was the encouragement he was giving me. It showed the warmth of the man.

"Because I know when I got on later myself, I was looking over my shoulder and saying 'that fella's after my place'. But Charlie was the opposite."

Whatever the best-laid plans of Higgins and his war cabinet were ("they had no alternative," reckoned the *Celt*, "but to drop Gallagher"), they were torn apart when Cavan came out flat and lifeless. Well before half-time, Charlie was thrown into the fray and seemed to have rediscovered that old zip. Towards the end of the game, he laid on a goal for Phil Murray as Cavan hung on to draw, 2-3 to 0-9.

The captain had the bit between his teeth again, the

Celt reporting that he "looked extremely fit again". He was training hard. That Tuesday, he lined out in the Cootehill tournament final and scored 0-8 in the Celts' 0-9 to 1-5 win over Ballyhaise.

And in the replay against Derry, with Carolan majestic at midfield, he shone in a slightly unconvincing 1-8 to 0-6 win.

"Derry really should have won that game in Clones, but they kicked an awful lot of wides," remembered Declan Coyle, a young seminary student from Mountnugent, who had broken into the team at full-forward.

"They simply didn't have the belief that they could actually beat Cavan. I remember talking to [Derry's] Tom Quinn and Malachy McAfee afterwards. They knew they let it slip but I re-assured them that there was no way that they would beat Down in the Ulster final — that we would not only beat Down but we'd hammer them. They agreed. Belief is a powerful thing."

So, it was Down again, for all the marbles.

¶ ¶ ¶ ¶

The All-Ireland and National League champions were red-hot favourites to retain their Ulster crown, with one bookmaker pricing them at 4/7 and installing Cavan as 4/1 underdogs.

But Down were worried. On the Thursday night at training, Sean O'Neill sensed it and gathered the players together in a circle. O'Neill gave that famous steely look and stared into each player's eyes.

"Who are we playing on Sunday?" he asked. His point was made.

On the Sunday, a crowd of 45,000 flocked to Casement Park and Cavan tore into the holders. Ten minutes before half-time, they were 0-7 to 0-2 up when Gene Cusack, who was marking the legendary Tom O'Hare, scored a brilliant goal ("By the age of 21," remembered wing-back Enda McGowan, "Cusack had put the fear of God into every full-back in Ulster. He destroyed Tom O'Hare in '69.") .

At the back, Kelly — then regarded as arguably the greatest right corner-back in history, who played his 17th match for Ulster the previous February — was on fire and Carolan and Newman dominated the midfield battle with McAlarney and Jim Milligan, as Cavan ran out 2-13 to 2-6 winners.

On the terrace, Vincent Pilkington had his eye on the clock. Moments before the whistle sounded, he made a break for it.

"When the game was over, I had timed it to a tee and I crossed the wire. And the great Andy McCabe, the Cavan corner-back, says to me 'Get off, son, the game's not over yet'.

"I was out in the middle of the field and then the whistle blew. I was looking for Charlie and I ran up and said to him, 'Charlie, you're a superman' or something like that. He says 'sure they wouldn't pass me the ball'," he laughs.

"But Charlie was past his best that year really."

A couple of minutes later, an official handed Charlie the Anglo-Celt Cup. A famous photo of the presentation exists; in it, Pilkington is leaning over his hero's right shoulder, straining to get close.

On the way home, Garrett O'Reilly remembers his father pounding on the steering wheel, "roaring and shouting" in celebration.

Garrett himself had missed out; he had been sitting his final exams, then broke an ankle and would only return to training before the All-Ireland semi-final against Offaly.

Down were sick.

"We should have known the history because Cavan were going to be truly, truly set for us and they certainly were. We were demolished in the sunshine in Casement Park that day," says McAlarney.

"It was a typical tigerish Cavan team that lined out that day. In those days you just got your one chance and if you weren't set for it, you were gone. In those days, you had to be set for your first-round match because you knew it was going to be a war. We were caught cold."

While Cavan were exultant, it was a different era. Most of the team didn't drink and the celebrations were nothing like what we have to come to expect today.

"Paddy Maguire had a taxi. He took me home from Casement along with Tom Lynch," recalled Coyle.

"We pulled up outside the Farnham Hotel on the main street. I opened the boot of the car to take out the bags with the boots and the togs. I lifted out the famous Anglo-Celt Cup. Paddy said: "Leave it back in the boot and I'll drop it up to Ray Carolan's during the week."

"The street was empty. Not a sinner out. After all, it was only the Ulster final, and you were expected to win that. What did you expect? A welcome home? Crowds? They tell me it was different in 1997 but then this was 1969.

"A man had walked on the moon. We had Woodstock. And we had the Anglo-Celt Cup back home where it belonged. I sat into Tom's Volkswagen Beetle and we headed up through Kilnaleck and Mountnugent, then up to Dungimmon."

¶ ¶ ¶ ¶

"On this form," wrote Peadar O'Brien in the *Press*, "the unpredictable Cavan side will make a tremendous bid in the All-Ireland series."

Offaly reached the All-Ireland final in 1961, which they lost by a point to Down, and had a number of survivors from that team — including the 'Iron man from Rhode', Paddy McCormack — and those veterans had been bolstered by graduates from their All-Ireland minor-winning team of '64.

They had beaten Kildare in the Leinster final and had been in fine form all season. Opinion was split as to who would advance to the final.

For one thing, there was little in the way of head-to-head meetings to go on. Cavan and Offaly had never met in the Championship, nor in a league game of any consequence since 1952. Even on the challenge game circuit, opening club pitches and so on, they had rarely, if ever, faced off.

The Faithful had torn through their province, racking up 3-14, 3-9 and 3-7 respectively in wins over Westmeath, Wexford and Kildare.

The national press was busy in expectation. TP, forever the optimist, reckoned the omens were good.

"Cavan have won an All-Ireland in every decade since the 1920s and this is their last chance to win one in the sixties," he said, getting ahead of himself.

Donegal captain Mickey McLoone was asked his thoughts and had no doubt where the key battleground lay.

"Cavan have Charlie Gallagher, their captain, fully fit and back in form again," reckoned McLoone.

"He will be tightly marked by Paddy McCormack but Charlie's opportunism should see him notch the vital scores."

The big question posed by the pundits was whether Cavan could reproduce their Ulster final form. In their previous three All-Ireland semi-final appearances, having trounced Down, they had failed to progress.

Kelly, for one, didn't buy it.

"There's no doubt," he said, "but that the Down jerseys seem to bring out the best in us. But I believe we can be as good against anyone else. We're a far better balanced side now and in the Ulster final all six forwards scored."

One of those, Gallagher, was still box office; three of the national papers illustrated their previews with his photo.

In the *Press*, he was asked if the trend of previous years would again prevail. His response was succinct.

"No," he said," it's far different this time."

¶ ¶ ¶ ¶

The Bogside was burning as Charlie skipped town. The rioting erupted at the end of an Apprentice Boys parade on August 12th and raged for three days.

Soon, the Catholic ghetto was barricaded and the British army were threatening to move in. The national population was under siege.

For training, Charlie got out of there. Adrian had been born a few months earlier and he, Maureen and the baby decamped to the Park Hotel in Virginia — Cavan's training was based in the town — for a week.

On August 24th, it was Croke Park and Offaly and a last chance, after 14 years, to be behind the band on All-Ireland final day.

When the teams arrived at Jones' Road for the match, which was televised live by RTÉ, they were greeted by torrential rain, which ceaselessly continued throughout the first half. The pitch was compared to an ice-rink.

The weather, though, is something of a forgotten aside around a match generally recalled for one reason only: the decision to take off Charlie Gallagher.

The exchanges were ferocious, bone-shaking. Offaly's defenders were renowned for their physicality, while Cavan played for their lives.

"At times, there was an almost alarming recklessness in the furious struggles for possession and an explosion always appeared to be imminent," reported Mick Dunne. "There were times when the onlookers were amazed that the tackling did not leave a line of cripples in its wake."

Offaly raced into a 0-5 to 0-1 lead but a goal from Hugh McInerney helped leave the sides level at half-time. Tony McTague, whose father was from Corlough in west Cavan, kept Offaly in the match and finished with a tally of 0-10, nailing every free-kick that came his way.

"I was the last man to mark Charlie in a county match," says McCormack, one of the most accomplished full-backs the game has seen.

"He had been around for years, the same as myself. He was one of the best corner-forwards in Ireland, even that time he was still very dangerous. He was tricky and determined and was just a great man to take a score."

As a child, McCormack had attended the 1952 All-Ireland final in which Cavan beat Meath and was an admirer of the Breffni men. But he only knew one way to play, as his nickname suggests.

"Whether Charlie liked the physical stuff or not, he was going to get it that day!" he smiles.

"That era was different. You got a rap when you were going for it, a rap when you got it and a rap when you were kicking it. And there were no remarks passed.

"There would have been fine-day footballers, top of the ground players, which you need as well. Charlie was probably that type of player. I used to shout at Charlie 'don't come in here!'. He was a nice guy but there wouldn't be much craic in a game like that, there was too much at stake in an All-Ireland semi-final.

"It's hard to get that far. When you did, you hit first and you asked questions after."

McCormack rated Gallagher as one of the very best he ever marked.

"Was I surprised he was taken off? Jaysus, of course I was. Charlie was THE man as regards scoring. We were told before we went out to make sure to watch him closely.

"It gave us a great boost when Charlie went off. He was one of the main danger men. But Cavan had a right team, a few great players.

"When they got that 14-yard free, I said to myself 'it's gone now anyway'. It didn't go over then and we were confident the second day, even though Cavan had great players.

"It would have been like us talking off Tony McTague. It would never have happened."

At the other end, Cavan were fluffing their lines. With eight minutes to go, the call was made. Gallagher was off, replaced by Micheál Greenan.

¶ ¶ ¶ ¶

A couple of minutes after Greenan came on, Cavan were awarded a 21-yard free, in front of the posts. Greenan stepped up but failed to rise the ball. It dribbled harmlessly towards the goals — some reports stated it went low and wide; others said an Offaly defender gathered and cleared. Regardless, it was a dreadful miss.

On the sideline, Charlie — who had scored in the region of 500 free-kicks for Cavan — looked on, helpless.

Cavan trailed by a point and launched a furious onslaught on the Offaly goal, missing two more gilt-edged chances. With two minutes to go, Gallagher was reintroduced.

Charlie's heir apparent, Cusack, eventually conjured the equaliser from nothing. And that was that. A first drawn All-Ireland semi-final since Down and Offaly — the sides with whom Gallagher's name is inextricably linked — in 1961.

The post-mortem immediately began.

"Cavan must have mourned the replacement of their free-taker-in-chief and captain Charlie Gallagher in the closing stages," said the Indo.

"Five minutes from the end, with Offaly leading 0-12 to 1-8, Cavan were awarded a free, which the Derry resident dentist would surely have pointed. In his absence, his replacement Micheál Greenan took the kick but his effort was doomed to failure from the moment the ball left his boot.

"Later, the Cavan selectors recanted their decision about Gallagher but another free did not come their way."

Said Paddy Downey in the *Times*: "Cavanmen will regret the decision which removed Gallagher from the field, for he would surely have scored from the free which Greenan missed."

Higgins was quoted in one newspaper explaining the logic.

"Charlie kept wandering out to the middle and was bringing his man with him," he said. "The trouble was that Paddy McCormack was doing the damage with his long ranging kicks."

Curiously, though, the manager said that he had not made the call to re-introduce his captain.

"I was down near the goals urging the boys on and I don't know whose decision it was."

Steve Duggan, not long out of his teens but close to Gallagher, could scarcely believe what he was seeing. And to this day, he still doesn't believe it was Higgins' doing.

"There were people shouting, and they weren't even selectors, to take off Charlie. Some of the ex-selectors and other people. And, by Jesus, Charlie was taken off and I don't even think Higgins knew about it.

"It was a huge decision. He might not have been having his greatest game but he would point frees from fifty yards out, no problem.

"He should never have been taken off. But it wasn't Higgins that did it. Higgins came down the line afterwards and said: 'Who took off Charlie?'

"It was a huge talking point at the time. Sure, *how* was he taken off? No-one knows who took him off. It was people shouting from the sideline and I remember that well."

Cavan's outstanding player on the day, centre-back Tom Lynch, feels Greenan was put in a tough position.

"I wouldn't blame him because he was only brought in off the line, a young fella. It was a wet, cold day. He shouldn't have been asked to take the free."

Said wing-back Enda McGowan: "Nobody knew what

happened. Micheál Greenan had only just come on and wasn't really into the game. It wasn't his fault. Nobody was to blame really."

Greenan was new and had been a brilliant addition to the side in the previous two years. Ironically, at a GAA-organised sports day earlier in the year, he had come first in place-kicking.

He went on to enjoy a long career as a referee and administrator but that free-kick still hangs over him.

"I still hear about it. It was my first kick of the ball and I slipped on my tail end. It was an awful wet day.

"The ball didn't go over the bar. People were saying Charlie would have scored it... and he possibly would have.

"It would have been a big decision at the time. I think what Higgins had in mind when he took Charlie off was that if there any frees, I might score them. But it was my first kick and my feet went from under me. I was about twenty-two."

The decision was the talk of the Gaelic football nation. Down had beaten Galway in a challenge match at a curtain-raiser and, a week later, The Connacht Tribune noted, in reference to Galway captain Seamus Leyden, that "the team management will not as yet have to 'do a Charlie Gallagher on him' and take him off in an important game."

To this day, even several of those who were on the field for Cavan are none-the-wiser as to what happened — or if they are, they don't want to rake over old coals.

"I remember, Mick spent a lot of the time in that game up at the Canal End goals," says Lynch. "He wasn't down at the dug-out with the selectors, I can remember that."

Gene Cusack has heard conflicting reports over the years.

"To this day, no-one has accepted responsibility. I still don't know who took him off. Different people say different things. I was a young fella at the time and I don't know."

Phil Murray watched it from the bench.

"I don't think he should have been taken off. Mick Higgins told me after the game that he wanted to put me on that day and the selectors said no. He came over to me and said it, 'Lightning, I wanted to put you on.'

"Charlie Gallagher shouldn't have been taken off. He was still a good footballer. Mick told me who made the call but I'm not naming any names. It's history now."

Carolan is of the same opinion. "It happened," he simply says, "so it happened."

Yet the man himself was philosophical about the whole thing.

"It was a match that could have been decided by a kick of the ball," Charlie told the *Press*.

"I think we threw away a few chances too many. After half-time I thought we could win and in the last few minutes, I was sure we were going to win. But that's football."

¶ ¶ ¶ ¶

The All-Ireland hurling final took place the following Sunday and then came the replay. Cavan were confident, even though the controversy over the drawn game and the substitution was still raging on.

"Was it a wise move," the *Celt* asked, "in taking off Gallagher, or was it panic stations?"

Carolan, in top form, had no doubts about the replay, though.

"I always thought we could win. If I went out with 14

schoolboys, I'd think we could win. It wasn't an illusion. It was the belief I had because I was used to winning," he once said.

The midfielder was a force of nature on his day and capable of controlling a match. He could not see how Cavan could lose the replay.

"I said to myself: 'We'll bloody beat these fellas the next day'. But it was another fierce wet day and we got beaten again."

Offaly banged in three goals and had the game won by half-time. A 48th-minute free from Charlie would prove to be his last-ever point in a Cavan jersey.

Cavan were out and, immediately, the realisation dawned. The 1960s were over and nothing would ever be the same again.

"We took that defeat very badly," said Lynch.

"It was the end of the road. It was like a morgue in Croke Park. Before that, it wasn't as bad but after that replay... To be beaten by not as good a team. Fellas were crying in the dressing-room. It was going to be very hard to pick it up."

The loss came 22 years to the day after Higgins had led Cavan to their third All-Ireland title in the Polo Grounds in New York, the city of his birth. He would never train a Cavan team again.

And at the county convention the following January, TP stepped down as chairman.

"He wouldn't have been satisfied," says Garrett, who didn't make it back on to the pitch that season.

"The four All-Ireland semi-final defeats of the '60s probably prompted him to retire. I would imagine so. He took them very bad, he'd be very down. He was child-like nearly with excitement when we beat Down in '67 and '69."

Kelly and Gallagher packed it in after a long innings. Lynch emigrated. The team and its support structure, painstakingly put together, quickly fell apart.

"Gabriel retired, Charlie retired and I went off. I travelled a bit. I went to Canada, I won a championship with Garryowen in Toronto. I used to play with Cavan in New York as well, I would fly down," says Lynch, wistfully.

As the tears fell on the concrete floor in Croke Park, nobody could have realised just how drastically things would change. Cavan would never again be a force at the elite level for a sustained period of time.

In the Cuchulainn GAA annual that December, journalist David Collins brought a sense of perspective to his playing career.

"Charlie Gallagher had the difficult task of trying to carry on the traditions of the great Cavan team of the 1945-54 era, since he and Gabriel Kelly came on to the Breffni team just as some of the greats were fading from the scene in the mid-'50s," he wrote.

"Many lesser players would have drowned in the mediocrity which followed Cavan's All-Ireland semi-final defeat in 1955 but although Cavan failed to win an Ulster title for the following seven years, Charlie still became a nationally-known figure.

"Consistently high annual scoring tallies showed him to be a man of class but fortune never saw fit to bestow even an All-Ireland final appearance on him."

His last line was sadly resonant.

"Nevertheless, Charlie's place in GAA history is secure,

especially, if as seems likely, he is the last of the great individual scoregetters from Breffni."

Other than those few paragraphs, there wasn't much made of Gallagher's retirement. Cootehill Celtic made a presentation of some crystal glasses to Charlie and Maureen but there were no statements, no eulogies.

It wasn't his style, or the done thing back then anyway.

"When he finished playing with Cavan, I'm sure he was disappointed but he would kind of throw his head back," says Maureen now.

Behind the shield of affability, though, he was hurting.

He gave an interview to the *Evening Press*, that they buried in a corner, and was unusually outspoken. The pain — of losing, of being taken off on such a big stage — drips from the page, even now.

"When a team is beaten in the championship, the selectors should start immediately rebuilding for the next one, whether that is through the Grounds tournament, National League or challenge games.

"In Cavan, the selectors have always tended to leave things too late. They start worrying about the Ulster Championship in May, this doesn't give a team enough time to knit into a championship side.

"I doubt," he concluded, "if I can be of any more use to Cavan."

SIXTEEN

Reality Check

Winter came down and a chill set in. The lifelong season rumbled on. There were fixtures to be fulfilled, appointments to be kept.

Charlie had been a starting senior inter-county footballer since before he was an adult. For him, things had suddenly and decidedly changed. Real life, away from the extended childhood of being an inter-county star, was beginning.

In December, the Cavanman of the Year awards were presented at a ceremony in Malahide. Traditionally, there were two annual winners; one cultural, one sporting. In '69, there were three — the usual two (which went to publican and tourism promoter Hugh Gough and young football sensation Gene Cusack) and a 'special award', which went to Gallagher.

"He was won practically every medal in football but the coveted All-Ireland one, which he richly deserved, has eluded him," read the citation.

He was still playing club football, which helped ease the transition to 'civilian' life. The awards were presented on Sunday, December 7th. Earlier that afternoon, Gallagher picked up a Junior Championship medal with Cootehill.

Having been regraded at the start of the year, when the main objection had been to Gallagher's presence, a young Cootehill side, with eight county minors, stormed to victory; the report noting that "this was a win engineered not by Gallagher but solely by a great team effort".

On Christmas Day, he turned 32. The following month, the Cootehill Celtic club recognised Charlie on his retirement. At a function in the White Horse Hotel — a humdrum affair which the *Celt* deemed worthy of a front page photograph — he and Maureen accepted a silver tea set.

And then came the annual county convention — a formal affair held in St Pat's over a weekend — at which Jim McDonnell took over as chairman and a letter was read out from TP O'Reilly, who had stepped down. Its tone was rueful. His time, he said, "was not as fruitful as we would have wished".

Viewed at a remove of 50 years, it is startling to witness how depressed football people were about the 1960s at its end but Cavan still held themselves to the highest standards. A decade without an All-Ireland title was viewed as a failure.

The fall-out from '69 was seismic. The Offaly defeat had sent tremors through the county — and then came the after-shocks. Even by the New Year and the convention, bad feeling still smouldered.

In February, Mick Higgins began to sift through the wreckage with an extraordinary statement at a county board meeting. Higgins had stepped aside not long after the Offaly loss but he hadn't intended on it being permanent.

"I have a few regrets on leaving," Higgins began.

"I am sorry for the players' sake that we did not win an All-Ireland. I am especially sorry for the older players such as Charlie Gallagher, Gabriel Kelly, Tom Lynch and JJ O'Reilly... The younger players have time on their sides and my sincere wish is that they will win not just one but a couple of All-Irelands.

"They were loyal to me and for that I am grateful. I hate ungratefulness. They were a lot more loyal to me than a lot of those around me were, but I did not know it at the time."

Higgins went on to list the sacrifices the players had made; training twice a week from January to June and four nights per week plus a match on Sundays thereafter.

"They gave their free time when they could be sitting back looking at TV or attending dances."

Before the Offaly game, they gave it everything, he said. One last shot maybe.

"Tom Lynch and Andy McCabe cut short their honeymoons so they could train. Phil Murray, although not sure of his place, was prepared to forfeit £40 of an air fare. Kelly gave up a trip to America. Brendan Donohoe turned down a job offer in Cork. Carolan, Newman, Tinnelly and Duggan abandoned holidays to be there and Gallagher spent his in Virginia, training.

"The persons who went behind my back, slated my methods — 'Oh, Higgins did so-and-so and lost an All-Ireland' — they are hypocrites and there are quite a few of them in this room tonight," he thundered.

The previous March, after a match against Sligo in Carrick-on Shannon, Higgins said, the players had held a meeting and requested that nobody — not even the chairman — bar themselves and Higgins should be allowed in the dressing-room before a match.

This policy subsequently caused problems further down the line. When Higgins wanted a break, the players asked for Kelly to train the side. Later, when it was time for Higgins to return, the same requests regarding the sanctity of the dressing-room had been repeated.

He had been happy with that but, he intimated, the new regime were not. His position was untenable.

And then, a thinly-veiled clarification about Gallagher.

"During the year, I never took off a player without consulting the selectors and all changes were made after consultation with them."

The room was stunned into silence. McDonnell thanked Higgins, his old comrade, and that was that. When it came to appointing selectors, Crosserlough delegate Tom Dowd proposed Gallagher for the role but later withdrew the suggestion.

¶ ¶ ¶ ¶

The months rolled on. In April, Gallagher scored 1-9 for Cootehill in the Drumgoon tournament. His brother, Brian, was by now training the team, who were operating at intermediate level. In the opening round of the championship, Charlie kicked 10 points in a win over Templeport and he added another five in the semi-final but they would lose next day out against Killygarry.

That June, Cavan, by now managed by Kelly, went into the championship with just eight survivors from the previous year's championship, with Kelly himself, Lynch, Hughie Newman, John Joe O'Reilly, Declan Coyle (studying for the priesthood) and Gallagher off the scene and Pat Tinnelly injured. They hammered Fermanagh, with Cusack scoring 1-5, but lost next time out to Derry.

One report described the Cavan attack as an "utter shambles". Down, meanwhile, were stunned by Antrim but lost the final to Derry, who — built around the 1965 St Columb's squad, along with the veteran Sean O'Connell among others — ended 12 years of Cavan and Down dominance.

Some consolation for the Intermediate Championship loss arrived for Cootehiill when they won the corresponding league, the final of which was not played until the following April, with Gallagher's controversial late penalty sealing the win.

"Gallagher had not one of his best games, although finishing top scorer with 1-5, and his best contribution came late in the game when he displayed some of his old fire," reckoned the *Celt*'s reporter.

That June, he came from Derry for a game in the Ballybay tournament, scoring 1-5; the match report singing the praises of "the one and only Charlie Gallagher".

Tournaments were a huge part of the football scene; Cootehill would win the Drumgoon one for the fourth successive year. The Celtics, famed for their expansive style, were always a big hit at the turnstiles and were in demand with organisers. Gallagher was still box office and his presence alone would add a couple of hundred to the gate.

In the next round in Ballybay against Monaghan side Truagh, he displayed that familiar magic, scoring 0-7 of Cootehill's 1-8.

"With a draw seeming almost certain," read the match report, "the referee awarded Cootehill a 40 yards free and informed former Cavan and Ulster star Charlie Gallagher that it was the last kick of the game... the ice-cool Charlie obliged by swinging the ball over the bar."

The tournament winners were each awarded a gold watch; this time, Cootehill lost to Donaghmoyne.

In the football heartlands, Gallagher's celebrity had not waned. If anything, given his appearances were confined only to club matches, it was growing. What's rare is wonderful.

The following month, he brought a Derry selection to play his home club in Celtic Park, Cootehill. The ground was jammed. Afterwards, the bars were too.

That September, another title arrived. Gallagher completed the set at club level when he helped Cootehill beat Virginia 2-8 to 1-3 to add the Intermediate Championship to his Senior and Junior Championship medals.

By now, though, he was reaching the end of the road. He had started to carry a little weight and wasn't really minding himself as he had. His sons, Adrian and Peter, had been born and Louise would soon follow. Business was booming and priorities were changing.

At the time, though, it was imperceptible. Maureen didn't notice any major shift in her husband's attitude now that he was a retired county player.

"Did he miss the football? Do you know, it's hard to know because at that stage you were starting family life."

¶ ¶ ¶ ¶

Charlie would continue to line out with his club, with some success, for another three years. After the Intermediate Championship success, he toyed with packing it in.

In December, 1971, Cootehill got to the Intermediate League final again, without him, and the *Celt* reported that he had "intimated he wouldn't be playing for a while".

But the sport of the chase is hard to resist. A week later, he came on as a sub in the decider. The flame still burned.

"Charlie Gallagher, so long the saviour of Cavan inter-county teams, stepped into the breech to save his club the ignominy of certain defeat," read the report.

Down by 1-3 to 0-1 at half-time against Killeshandra, the Celtics threw Gallagher in and he scored five points to rescue a draw. The headline said it all: "Still a star".

Cootehill won the replay. Retirement was put on ice for another while and in 1972, he was re-energised, turning in a string of good displays. He was approaching his 20th year in the famous green and white hoops and his status still hadn't dimmed, nor had the excitement his arrival for matches would generate.

"Absence makes the heart grow fonder," says Kevin Óg Carney.

"Charlie being in Derry and coming home for games possibly added to his legendary status among myself and my peers and others around the town. It was like you had this icon on loan and you were able to call on his services when they were most needed."

In June, he played in the Jimmy Magee Radio/TV All-Stars match at Ballinagh alongside the likes of Higgins, Phil 'The Gunner' Brady, Tony Tighe, Willie Doonan, Larry Cunningham and Fr Michael Cleary.

His form for Cootehill was good but, from nowhere, he was named on the Cavan panel for the Ulster Championship opener against Monaghan that June.

Still just 33 but having played so much football, he was described as "the ageless Charlie Gallagher" in one report.

In the end, he didn't tog out as Cavan beat Monaghan, watching the game from the terrace and declining to comment to the pressmen on his inclusion in the panel.

Shorn of the rhythms of the season to which he has become accustomed, the years were flying by quicker now. Cootehill were seen as an up-and-coming team, young guns, and he the wizened, wily veteran. They were back among the big boys and fancied to make waves.

In January, 1973, came a memorable day as they defeated Cornafean to win the Senior League title for the first time since 1957. A photo in the *Celt*, under the heading 'Big Three help Cootehill to success' showed Sean Foy, flanked by Gallagher and 1950s player John Joe Tierney — "who captained Cootehill in the 1950s when Gallagher came into the team at the age of sixteen" — all suited and booted after the match.

By that July, he turned in a Man of the Match performance with 10 points in a championship win over Arva. Next up were Crosserlough, the greatest Cavan club side of them all, who were aiming for an eighth Senior Championship in a row.

In the quarter-final, inspired by Gallagher's 0-7, Cootehill ended their reign and they were immediately installed as the hottest of favourites to win back the title they had last held in 1955. Gallagher was playing his best football in years.

Down by four points against Ramor United in the semi-final, Charlie kicked four in a row.

"The equaliser," it was reported, "came amid a great roar when Gallagher kicked a magnificent point from all of 50 metres."

In the replay, though, Cootehill lost by 3-10 to 0-17 after

extra-time. Despite a haul of 0-11 from their 34-year-old full-forward, another summer was gone.

There was one last hurrah. Charlie didn't play again for six months but, by May of '74, Cootehill were "hopeful" he would yet return. Losing by three points with 10 minutes to go in the league final against Cavan Gaels, they threw him in. The Gaels were rattled, panicked. Cootehill won by two.

"I wasn't at the game," recalls Cavan Gaels player Paddy Reilly, who was recovering from a broken leg. "But I well remember the talk afterwards. Charlie Gallagher had turned the match for Cootehill."

But, in the championship, they lost to Woodford Gaels, an amalgamation from west Cavan. Charlie played at full-forward and didn't score.

Time had caught up with him at last and he hung up his boots, once and for all.

¶ ¶ ¶ ¶

Born the son of a doctor in Market Street, Cootehill. Educated in the local national school and, later, St Patrick's College in Cavan. Charlie Gallagher and John Charles McQuaid had more in common than one would imagine.

McQuaid was born in 1895 and, by 1940, had risen to become Catholic Primate of Ireland and Archbishop of Dublin.

In 1972, McQuaid, described in the title of one tome as "the ruler of Catholic Ireland", retired. A year later, his friend Eamon De Valera stepped down as President. Both men had lost relevance. The country was changing, fast.

The closed, almost puritanical society that they had led was beginning to be dismantled.

For modern Ireland, it was the end of the beginning. For Charlie Gallagher, maybe the opposite was true. Like Dev and his fellow Cootehill man, Charlie was now retired. The power all three wielded was, essentially, gone.

¶ ¶ ¶ ¶

Football made him and football broke him. Charlie was wedded to the game and the divorce was messy.

Derry City was a soccer town; Gaelic activity was minimal. Charlie was cut off from the source of his celebrity, to the point where his younger children, Peter and Louise, would not have been all that aware of his status in the game.

His eldest, Adrian, was. He overheard stories in hotels and bars, especially around Cootehill. Sometimes, he would accompany his dad to the All-Ireland final in Croke Park.

"I would have been aware in Croke Park of him talking to everybody and having a special sort of status, knowing that he was popular," Adrian says.

But in later years, Charlie was never good at keeping in contact with old comrades — or old foes, for that matter. On his occasional trips to matches, he approached with a degree of wariness that wasn't in keeping with his generally open personality.

"He wouldn't have been relishing the contact he would have with people on match days," explains Adrian.

"I wouldn't say apprehensive but he wouldn't have been embracing the whole thing. I think there was a lot going on in his subconscious with regard to that and when he had a few jars, that would have come to the fore. Then, he welcomed the whole chat and reminiscing and celebrity side of things and would talk for hours. But on an ordinary day, no, he wouldn't mention football."

¶ ¶ ¶ ¶

Derry City in the 1970s was a mean scene. There was blood on the streets. People looked for refuge. Some found it in politics, or in the war. Others in sport. Some just got out and many found what they were looking for in the bottle. If you were that way inclined, drinking partners were never scarce.

"That was a different time in Derry," says Msgr McQuillan.

"A lot of people were drinking; everybody was sort of drinking. It was a tough time. People were looking for a means of escape in a way.

"If you were walking down the street and you saw a car parked somewhere, you would walk over to the other side before you'd pass it. There were murders. It was fairly dark. That would have caused people to drink, people would drink in houses until early in the morning. Or late in the morning. "

That drinking culture, like the Nationalist community in general, was entrenched.

"It was just untrue," says John Cully, whose father was 15 years Gallagher's senior.

"I can remember the parties in the house, all Dad's professional friends. In the '50s, the '60s, there was a whole culture of drinking.

"People my dad's age would have grown up in the thirties and things would have been difficult and suddenly there was a flow of money and affluence beginning. They would go out a few nights a week. Charlie would have been with a different, younger set, I'd say."

Maureen Gallagher remembers how people "went to houses and had parties". That was the social scene.

The city itself was a war zone. The army had been deployed and there were running battles. Riots were commonplace — they broke out a couple of hundred metres from Clarendon Street and the CS gas would waft through the windows of the surgery — and death stalked the banks of the Foyle. Bombings were a regular soundtrack; atrocities were commonplace.

Poverty was not an issue for Charlie, who had a good job. While most of his patients were from the NHS, many of them on social welfare, he had built up a private practice on the side and was particularly popular in Inishowen, across in Donegal. Patients loved him.

One, a man named Noel McLaughlin, wrote a poem in his honour, addressing it to "Charlie G, Le Dentist Terrible". He was well-known in Gaelic football circles, obviously, but his gift for mixing, for attracting people, knew no bounds.

In time, he made friends — and patients — from all areas. The predominantly-Unionist rugby crowd was one unlikely base.

"There was very little integration that time," says McQuillan, "but, ah, Charlie was so likeable, most creeds liked him, put it like that."

Charlie, Maureen and family lived in Ardmore parish, two miles out of the city, in a comfortable home. He sang informally in the church choir. Gallagher should have had the world at his feet but those feet were now all-but-redundant — he was a former inter-county star.

"Charlie couldn't come to terms with his career ending, he couldn't come to terms with being AN Other, an ordinary guy. He missed the flag of 'howya Charlie'," says Frankie Kennedy.

"Other great footballers had been the same. A hero of yesterday. Never adjusted. Sport is great but when it's over you've got to be yourself and keep sport in its place. Charlie garnered such heroism and took it to his heart and thought it was a reality. But as you stop playing, you discover you're yesterday's man and nobody gives a damn."

While the family got on with life and were never involved in any sort of politics, the Troubles were unavoidable. A bomb across the road, in a water tower, once blew in the windows of their home. Charlie once felt threatened in a pub — someone tipped him off, a word to the wise, that he could be in danger. On another occasion, a story went around that he had been taken out.

"I was only a child at the time," says Derry native Kevin MacDermott, a journalist whose father, a doctor, was a friend and colleague.

"I clearly remember this rumour going around one day. And there was almost out-and-out war. Shooting a man like Charlie, who was so popular, would have been crossing the Rubicon."

Day-to-day life was difficult — checkpoints, blasts, killings. In 1976, Maureen's car was hijacked.

It was a beautiful summer's day and she had left three-year-old Louise with a child-minder, dropped Charlie back to work after his lunch and headed into town to do some shopping. She took a shortcut through the staunchly pro-IRA Bogside at three o'clock in the afternoon when two gunmen stopped her car.

"One fella got into the back and put something to my neck. The other fella got into the front and put a gun to my knee. And all he said was 'drive!'"

Maureen was directed to Capel Street, past men in vests sunning themselves and into a backyard off the beaten track.

"I can still see this boy with rimless glasses standing at the back door of the car. Derry was small enough, you nearly would have known them to see. And I didn't know these two boys.

"Out they got and opened the boot. And they went into the house and came out and asked me for my licence. And they said: 'What the fuck are you living in the Waterside for with a name like that? Who are you?'

"And they went back in and came out. I think what they were trying to do was get this boat motor I had belonging to my brother out of the boot and I don't think they were able to.

"I said to them: 'Look, I have a child with a baby-sitter and they'll be worrying' and he said 'none of your soft talk'. And at this stage I started crying. That was worse!

"In again they disappeared. I remember the heat was beating down and I was shaking. And they came out and I said: 'You know my husband works about a quarter of a mile from here'.

'Who's he?'

"And as soon as I said 'Charlie Gallagher' and there was no recognition, I knew they were strangers.

'Well,' I said, 'we were at Martin McGuinness's house only two weeks ago. My husband is a dentist and he had to do a house-visit to Martin McGuinness's mother. I sat in the car and he went in.'

"In they went again but this time, whatever they were told, they came out and said to me 'keep your mouth shut and go!'

"I don't remember reversing out of that place. And I phoned Charlie and he laughed! He says 'you're joking!'; I said 'I'm not'. Whenever I mentioned McGuinness, that was it. They went and checked."

That night, the Odeon Cinema was blown up. The bomb had been placed in the boot of a car.

¶ ¶ ¶ ¶

It felt, in time, like he was an actor playing the role of Charlie Gallagher, the man who had it all. One night, in a taxi from a bar with a young couple, they hit a checkpoint. The army ordered them out and asked for a date of birth.

"Myself and the late JC, that will do you," said Charlie, a Christmas Day baby. It was a favourite wisecrack of his. He was taken away in a Saracen and spent the night in the cells at Strand Road barracks.

"He was like that, he thought he could get away with things like that and most of the time, he did," says Maureen, smiling.

That was one of the funnier incidents. Others were sombre.

Alcohol had stalked him and as the years went on, it grabbed him and wouldn't let go. The tightest marker of all and the one he couldn't shake off. First, football was everything and then, the football and the drinks after. In time, the 'everything' faded and the drink became the only thing.

By the late 1970s, the familiar trips home had dried up. It is a big ask for a man with a child-like approach to life to suddenly grow up. Football is a game to be played but real life is no toy.

Addicts find solace in routine and their condition is aggravated when that routine is broken. Sometimes, after a match, Charlie would stay in Cootehill till Monday morning and have a drink — the cure — before heading back up the road. Other days, he returned after the game but made some pit stops along the way.

Solace. Routine. Those same signs above the door, same as always. The Farnham. Packie Eddie Lynch's, Connolly's. Down the road, Gerry McCormack's, Flood's. McIver's. Comforting places, places where a man like Charlie Gallagher would find a warm welcome and a cold bottle, high praise on a high stool.

Football was gone and took that away with it. In February, 1979, Charlie's father died. By then, only Brian was in Cootehill. Life began to centre on Derry in its entirety.

After he finished playing, Charlie had written to the Ulster Council asking for two tickets for the Hogan Stand on All-Ireland final day. They refused. He wrote again and called and eventually, a solitary ticket arrived and, scrawled on the accompanying note were the words "don't tell anybody". That hurt.

The years flew. The children were getting bigger. Despatches reached home that Charlie had been drinking a lot. Reports were sketchy. One former teammate would call to see him and found him, on one occasion, in a daze in a bar.

"There was a fella here used to travel for Whelan's boot shop and he used to keep me informed about Charlie, the odd time he'd see him," says Foy sadly.

"He came in this day and he told me he had been in Derry and he saw five or six of these corner boys sitting drinking bottles on the street and Charlie was in the middle of them. Another day, he said he didn't belicve his eyes; Charlie copped him and he went up an entry out of the way."

In 1984, seeking a clean break, Charlie moved home and set up a practice in his brother's surgery. His nephew Francis helped him get the place ready.

"Francis said it was the best summer of his life," Charlie's daughter Louise recalls.

"He helped daddy get the whole surgery set up and he never stopped laughing."

The local football community were overjoyed at his return. Soon, he was roped into training the Celtics' Under 21 footballers and was photographed attending a couple of county board meetings as a delegate.

Around this time, Larry McCluskey met his old teammate on a walk out the Station Road. Maureen and the children were coming down for the weekend — they would soon move permanently — and he was "very pleased and jovial about that."

But it couldn't last. The disease was rampant and overpowering. He began to drink again, surreptitiously.

McCluskey had visited Charlie in Lincoln Place when his idol was a student in Dublin, a guinea pig of sorts for a trainee dentist. He found him "affable and competent", senior in the group and well-liked.

Once or twice, he witnessed Charlie stroll into the Metropole Ballroom in O'Connell Street, where "he cut a dash as he made his away along one side of the ballroom".

But that had changed the next time he sat in his chair, in Bridge Street, Charlie's final surgery.

"The quality of his dental work, attendance and concentration was slipping — he hooked my lip as he removed a dental instrument. We both laughed but also recognised, the sharpness of the Dental College of 25 years before had blunted."

Now in his late 40s, Charlie was drinking heavily, his handsome face bloated.

James Brady last saw him in the Market Square in Cavan, on match day. At one time, when they were young and anything was possible, the pair had had lined out together in the full-forward line for school, college and county; James setting them up, Charlie knocking them down. Those days were gone forever.

"I went up to some match Cavan were playing and he was coming walking down the street with two other mates after the match and they were singing and he was well jarred. And that was the last time I saw him alive."

One teammate bumped into him by chance and saw an opportunity to bring him back into the fold.

"Charlie never got over finishing up the football," he says.

"He didn't move on and you have to. Young fellas don't know who we are now and you just have to accept that.

"I was walking out of Breffni Park after a match and I met Charlie. He had a few jars on him. I went over and started talking to him and I wasn't sure if I was getting through to him.

"'Charlie, did you ever try the golf?' I said, 'I'm playing it, I'm no good at it but it's a good hobby, you should come out with us.'

"Charlie looked at me for a couple of seconds and I thought he was considering it. And then he just said: 'Do you remember the time we played Down and you sent down a long ball and I put it over the bar?' He never moved on."

Some one-time friends and teammates now kept their distance. The hangers-on were gone, too.

Kennedy adored his friend and tells a tale with an ache in his voice.

"I heard that he came to a championship match on a wet day in Breffni Park. I didn't see him. He was standing up, away up on the hill with an old coat and a hat, on his own. Nobody went near him."

SEVENTEEN

The Knock

Maureen Gallagher was in bed when she heard the knock. Four eventful years had passed since Charlie, with his family, returned to Cootehill. It was a Monday evening.

The country was basking in a heat-wave. In Clones, venue for the Ulster final, a meteorological station recorded an average temperature that month of over 20 degrees, much higher than normal.

In some parts of the country, that July was the hottest on record and by the middle of the month there was a drought. Farmers were worried but for the rest, it was glorious. Adults and children flocked to well-known swimming spots and each day, the newspapers carried photos of families frolicking in the sun. The press was full of warnings, too, though. There had been 29 deaths by drowning that summer.

"There was a heat-wave that July. We used to walk out to the river. That particular evening, I had a cough and I said to him, 'I'm not going out'," remembers Maureen.

"I remember thinking 'I'll just go to bed early'. So, off he went."

¶ ¶ ¶ ¶

When Charlie had first returned to Cootehill, things had gone well and he quickly built up a trade.

With Brian's help, Charlie had stopped drinking and gotten back into the football scene. In '85, he trained the Cootehill Under 21 team. Soon, he was on the club's committee, attending county board meetings and popped up here and there around the county, when asked, presenting medals to various juvenile teams.

"It brought a great lift to the town and to the club when Charlie returned to Cootehill," says Carney.

"We hadn't won a Senior Championship since the mid '50s and people hoped that maybe this iconic player from the recent past was coming back and was going to be the Messiah and resurrect us and would have the same Midas touch off the field as he did on it.

"Charlie would have been hugely enthusiastic about the club when he came home and I remember him coming down to the pitch and taking penalties in his civvies after training. He was always a bubbly, effervescent character — players loved to see him coming down. I never saw him without a smile on his face. Just a very warm personality and hugely popular."

But the disease was still gnawing at him. After some time, he was drinking again.

¶ ¶ ¶ ¶

On Christmas Day, 1988, Charlie turned 50. He had packed a lot into his half-century; been through a lot and survived, the worse for wear, maybe, but surviving and still beloved. But he had less than seven months to live.

By now, the alcohol had him in its grip. He had tried to shake it but, just as on the football field, he was a marked man. The difference was that now, the old magic was impotent.

At one point, he checked in to St Davnet's, a psychiatric hospital in Monaghan Town, to dry out. McCluskey and he had never been close but Larry called to visit and found him "the centre of attention, in the centre of a small group of men, sharp as a button, entertaining them with much laughter".

Foy's shop remained a focal point for football chat, idle gossip and craic. A place where men gathered and time passed quickly.

"Three or four days before he died, he came down and got his hair cut," said Foy.

"I had always cut his hair when he'd be in town. I mean, it was an honour.

"He would have been well 'Killarneyed'. He said his father was the most decent man in this town."

Even with drink on board, Charlie rarely if ever lost his temper. Now aged 51, he was floating along, a bottle here, a half-one there. Some errands to see to, his hair to be cut. He left Foy's shop and went about his business.

That was the last time Foy would see his old comrade alive.

¶ ¶ ¶ ¶

Charlie's last journey on foot took him past the football grounds, Hugh O'Reilly Memorial Park, named after the great player and manager; the rebel who came to Cootehill on the run and made the place famous as a football town before Gallagher brought it to a new level.

On he went, heading for Scarvy Bridge.

Decades earlier, there had been another famous bathing spot in Cootehill. It was also on the winding Annalee River but up a stretch, out at the townland of Lislea. But in July of 1955, a teenager had died in the water there and local mothers stopped allowing their children to swim the spot.

In time, Scarvy Bridge, a mile and a half out the Mountain Lodge Road, became the place where Cootehill people went to cool off when the weather was hot, even though it was known that there were treacherous pockets there; deeper points, where danger lurked. Just a week earlier, a teenager had been rescued after getting into difficulty in one.

That evening, a good crowd of locals were out at Scarvy, along a stretch of land owned by a local farmer named Robert McCrea. Charlie wandered out in no particular hurry.

After a while, the crowd thinned out and all that were left were Charlie, a very strong swimmer, and a few youngsters down the way a little.

¶ ¶ ¶ ¶

Back on Cavan Street, Maureen heard the knock.

"I was in bed at about ten o'clock and the banging came to the door and I thought 'he's forgotten his key'. And I ran down the stairs and here was our local Canon standing at the door.

"The Canon, kind of, stepped in and put his arm on my shoulder and he says: 'Maureen, Charlie's missing at the river.'

"'Ah, he's gone into town,' I said, 'and he's probably in

one of the pubs.' 'No,' he said, 'his wee dog is sitting on his clothes.'

"So then, of course, the alarm bells were going."

Night was falling. Soon, sirens sounded and the river bank and the old stone bridge were intermittently illuminated — blue and white, blue and white, those old familiar colours.

¶ ¶ ¶ ¶

Raymond McMullen and a couple of girls, Linda Foy and Catherine Swift, were also at the river that evening. Ray was driving and Charlie asked him for a lift. "Sure," said Ray. "No bother."

By now, everyone else had left.

"Charlie had been in for his dip, came out again and shouted to Ray 'I'll take a lift in'. And he got in again," said Maureen. "And they waited and they waited."

The trio heard what sounded like a struggle and, looking back, saw that Charlie was in trouble. In a panic, they sprinted back to the river but he had gone down. Soon, he re-emerged and then disappeared again. The light was fading.

"And they ran like hell, he [Ray] had to run over two fields to get to the road. And they raised the alarm.

"They found him in 26 feet of water."

At 12.05pm, the body was discovered, about 200 yards downstream. The bright day was long gone, replaced by a chill in the air. A doctor arrived, Dr Gerard J White, and made the necessary pronouncement. Charlie Gallagher was dead.

¶ ¶ ¶ ¶

Back in town, on Bridge Street, Foy was standing outside his premises. He'd been cutting hair all day as the sun beamed in the window and he was tired. The drowsy scene, all of a sudden, became charged.

"This young fella, Ray McMullen, came out of the car and ran past me and into his own house, he lived next door to me.

"I said, 'Woah! What's the excitement about?' and he never looked round at me. It must have been a half an hour after when somebody came and rapped the window and said Charlie Gallagher was drowned."

Around the same time, Kevin Óg Carney was coming home from work. Carney was a young staff reporter with the fledgling Cavan Leader. As a child, he could vividly remember the crowds gathering on street corners in anticipation of Charlie's arrival home.

As a man, he was now confronted with the same scene, identical but all too different.

"In the Leader, you finished up late on a Monday night. It was a bright summer's evening and there were people on the corners; four or five here, four or five there.

"I knew straight away that there was something serious had happened. I felt the vibes coming into the town, there was something unsettling about the place. That was the scene that greeted me."

That night, the barber barely slept. At day-break, as soon as he heard the birds chirping, he arose.

"As soon as I woke up, all I could think about was Charlie. And I said, 'I'll go out and see where this happened', it was about seven o'clock in the morning, a lovely bright morning.

"I went out and got out of the car and walked onto the field. I remember I found a five-pound note lying on the grass which had fallen from somebody's pocket. Just an ordinary morning but a terrible day."

¶ ¶ ¶ ¶

The first of the national newspapers to pick up the story were *The Evening Press* and *The Evening Herald,* both of which ran it on their front pages with separate photos of Charlie. The picture chosen by the *Press* was taken in 1969 and was tightly cropped, showing only that perfectly Brylcreemed hair, dark eyes, thin lips and a white shirt collar. The dead man was, reporter Damian McHugh noted, "a very popular figure".

The *Leader* had been established a few years earlier to take on the established *Anglo-Celt.*

A tabloid, the *Leader* went big on the story, splashing it across several pages. For Carney, making his way as a journalist, it was a hellishly difficult 'marking'. He was the local man, he had the contacts and could pull together background and tributes. But Gallagher was a friend and his idol.

"I was only in the business of journalism a year at that stage. The late Eugene McGee was editor of the *Cavan Leader* and he didn't ask me to cover it now; he told me to cover it. I wasn't in news really, I was in sports but he directed that I cover it and I didn't want to and I told him that but I had no choice.

"So, I covered it as best I could. It was surreal, definitely. It was someone that ought not to be to be dead. It was a crime that he had died.

"It's the only obituary I have ever written. I have been asked to do others but I wouldn't. I took far longer I'm sure than Eugene McGee wanted me to but in my mind it deserved to run for weeks and weeks, the news of his death. It was the hardest thing I ever had to write, without a shadow of a doubt. Nothing else compares."

The *Celt*, as would be expected, also covered the death and the funeral in detail, reporting verbatim on county board chairman Peter's Brady's graveside oration.

"It has often been said," eulogised Brady, "in relation to the Irish that all their sons are merry, all their songs and sad and all their heroes are dead.

"We could, at least in the case of Charlie Gallagher, reflect that we did not delay until he was no longer of this world to reflect on his talent and genius.

"When we think of Gaelic football played at its skilful best, let us think of Charlie Gallagher. When we think of honour and pride in wearing our colours, let us think of Charlie Gallagher.

"When we think of the commitment necessary to achieve success, let us think of Charlie Gallagher.

"When we think of the highest standards of sportsmanship, let us think of Charlie Gallagher.

"And when we come to coach our young people in all that is best in our national games, let us always think of Charlie Gallagher."

Elsewhere, old colleagues were asked for their memories.

"I knew him from when he was a first year student in St Patrick's College and played with him right through UCD and with Cavan up to the 1960s," Jim McDonnell was quoted as saying.

"I feel that he was one of the best-ever Cavan forwards and was mad about the game. He lived for nothing else, only football."

Said Mick Higgins: "Charlie was a gentleman on and off the field, a sportsman first and last."

Journalist Eamonn Gaffney, referring to the Sunday People's headline in 1967 — 'Charlie Is Cavan's Darling' — said: "No other phrase could sum up Charlie Gallagher so concisely and so realistically.

"He was a man who never quite grew up and he enjoyed his status as the popular legend he was in his heyday."

Writing in the Star that Friday, columnist Michael Hand described him as "a beautiful footballer, stylish and swift".

"I knew him well. The last time we met was in a cold graveyard in the Bogside of Derry at the funeral of the Bloody Sunday victims."

The Sunday papers were laden with tributes, too. Enda Colleran, captain of Galway in 1965 and 1966, told the *Sunday Independent* that Gallagher was "so deceptive and skilful, so deadly with the body-swerve and had such a great positional sense that I rate him one of the most difficult — if not the most difficult — corner-forwards I ever came up against".

¶ ¶ ¶ ¶

Those tributes provide a warm glow but it wears off quickly. In the weeks afterwards, there was little mention of Charlie Gallagher in newsprint or on the airwaves. People moved on but for the Gallagher family nothing would ever be the same.

At the time of their father's death, just one of the Gallagher children, middle-child Peter, was at home. He had just completed his Leaving Cert in the local secondary school, St Aidan's.

Louise, then 16, was in America, having gone over to help her cousin mind children during the summer holidays. And Adrian, 19, was in London, where he had gone with a friend to work, painting on the underground. In the end, Adrian would return to the UK and spend over 10 years working there.

While they dabbled in the game and did well in other sports — Peter was an accomplished cyclist, his dad buying him his first racing bike when he was 15 — neither of the boys ever really got into football.

"My father never, ever pushed us into football," says Peter. "I suppose it would have been hard to follow in his footsteps."

And, in any case, circumstances changed.

"He died in July and I was starting college that September. We had no income then, so I worked every weekend and hadn't time for football anyway."

Few of Charlie's medals — Sigerson Cups, County Championships, Ulster Championships or Railway Cups — sit on display in Maureen's home in Cootehill. Many of them, he simply handed away over the years.

"I saw him giving Railway Cup medals away in Derry," she says.

"I remember when we got engaged, I had bought him a watch and chain. He used to wear it in his breast pocket. And he had the Railway Cup medals all attached and they were the ones I saw him taking off and handing over.

"And, of course, the ones who took them were worse. But he had no care at all for stuff like that. None."

"He had the memories," says Louise, "and after that, he didn't care."

¶ ¶ ¶ ¶

The inquest into the death of Charlie Gallagher took place 20 years to the week after Cavan had lost the All-Ireland semi-final replay to Offaly in Croke Park. To that point, Cavan had won 38 Ulster titles. Charlie never wore the blue jersey again after those games against Offaly and by the time of the inquest, the county was still awaiting its 39th title.

Inquests at the time were usually held in the courthouse in Cavan Town, or the Town Hall. This one took place in the latter. They were semi-regular; a handful of deaths would be grouped together, a coroner would hear the medical evidence and a jury would, usually, accept what the experts had said and rule accordingly.

In attendance would be the witnesses, the jury, the coroner — in this case, local solicitor John V Kelly — and members of the family.

The practice at the time was that a jury would be rounded up from the ranks of courthouse staff. And that is how Micheál Greenan, the teammate who had come on for Charlie Gallagher in his second last match and missed the free that would have sunk Offaly, ended up present on the jury inquiring into Charlie's death, two decades later.

"With any accidental death, there's usually an inquest," says Greenan. "I would have sat on a number of them over the years. The guards would come in looking for a few people in the courthouse.

"The inquest is usually based on the medical evidence and you wouldn't know who the cases were going to be when you'd go in. There could be four or five of them. That day, Charlie happened to be one of them.

"The rest of them on the jury wouldn't have known Charlie but, of course, I did. It could be anyone from County Cavan. Charlie's happened to come up that day."

The guard, the doctor, the fireman, the people who tried to save him, all spoke. The coroner said the county had lost a great footballer, a man who could score points from any angle with either foot.

And then the jury returned their verdict: "In accordance with the medical evidence, death by asphyxia caused by accidental drowning".

The book was closed and the people filed out in silence.

EIGHTEEN

Song And Story

MJ Clarke was having a drink with a friend, Paddy Far-relly, and talk turned to football, as it usually does. One of MJ's earliest memories of the game was attending the Ulster final in 1969; the sun shining in Casement, the bus honking its horn through towns on the way home. Down toppled. And Charlie, lifting the cup.

"Anyone who was there that day still remembers it... it was one of those JFK moments," he says.

So, MJ and Paddy were in a local bar when Paddy piped up.

"It's unbelievable," he said, "that nobody ever wrote a song about Charlie Gallagher."

MJ, a popular local radio presenter got home and broke out his guitar and started working on some lyrics. Within 20 minutes, he had put together the bones of Charlie From Cootehill. He got on to Eddie Fitzsimons, a friend and football follower from Gowna. They hired a studio in Mullingar and a producer called Paul Sheerin and added the meat.

That was early in 1993. The song took off.

"It started to get picked up on the local radio stations because Charlie was as well-known as sliced bread. He was so well-liked across the board, even from people who weren't interested in sport," said Clarke. "It started to get airplay."

The song was released on cassette in May. By September, it had reached New York, where it was a huge hit, featuring on Irish programmes broadcast by the local stations. Soon, it had been noticed by a producer in Nashville who added something else.

"Another great football supporter called Charlie Clerkin was doing an album and he recorded it as well and included it on an album called *The Gallant Men of 1947*, which is sort of self-explanatory. "Then, yet another great football supporter, Ian Corrigan, who had an absolutely huge hit with a song called *The Gallant John Joe*, recorded it. He knew Charlie, too, and he was the third person to record it... I must say, I was very pleased about it. And that's how I became a millionaire!"

The song quickly entered the canon. In 1997, Cavan won their first Ulster Championship since '69 and later played Kerry in New York to commemorate the 1947 Polo Grounds final. Football nostalgia was in the air; *Charlie From Cootehill* could be heard ringing out in the bars of Woodlawn and Sunnyside and the other Irish enclaves, night and day.

"It was very popular. Most of the proceeds went to various charities, it wasn't a money-making venture at all. It was just a gesture to one of the greatest sporting heroes; he would have been the George Best of Gaelic football, or the Ronaldo, or Maradona."

Later, MJ and Eddie were invited on to RTÉ Radio's *Both Sides Now* show to talk about Gallagher. The poet and writer Brendan Kennelly was a guest on the same show and, before they went on air, in the green room, the men fell into talking.

"Brendan asked us what we were doing up there. Oh

Lord, he knew more about him than we did, even though he came from Kerry. Charlie was just one of these people who really made an impact.

"He was everybody's hero. He *was* the Georgie Best of Gaelic football. Unbelievable. The *Sunday Independent* used to run a list of Ireland's leading scorers every week and Charlie was on top of that for years.

"Thirty years ago, maybe we were more easily pleased, but Charlie was the boy. I often think the GAA should have put up a monument to him in Cootehill. There was nothing really — gone and forgotten.

"Only for that bit of a song that we clapped together in twenty minutes, there wouldn't be a word about him. There should be more recognition for guys like that; they were the backbone of the cultural and sporting life in the country. Everybody knew Charlie Gallagher."

To this day, there is no statue to honour his memory in his hometown, where the club grounds are named after Hughie O'Reilly.

"In some regards, Charlie's status would, maybe, have suffered from the fact that Hughie O'Reilly was an adopted son of Cootehill and was associated with all five of Cavan's All-Ireland winning teams," says Kevin Óg Carney.

"That was a hard act to follow. Hughie was Mr GAA in Cootehill and Hughie was alive all through Charlie's best years. He was there, present in the town, and he and his brother, Tommy, were huge figures in the GAA there.

"But in terms of legacy, for two generations at least, everybody wanted to be Charlie Gallagher. He was number one — above the soccer stars and everyone else. In Cootehill, he was the pin-up ahead of world stars.

"The club was struggling to win anything in the '70s

and '80s and Charlie's legacy would have given sustenance to a lot of players, including myself, in terms of what they could aspire to. Very few players from Cootehill represented Cavan in the years from his retirement to his death so, without him, there would have been no iconic figure there to look up to."

¶ ¶ ¶ ¶

Two years after his death, some Cootehill Celtic stalwarts in London got together and had the idea of running an inter-county tournament in Cootehill to honour Gallagher's memory. It ran for a couple of seasons, the big guns of the day — Donegal, Dublin — taking part. In 1992, future All-Ireland-winning manager Jim McGuinness picked up the Man of the Match award in the final.

The sport moved on. Cavan rose again, briefly, in the mid-1990s, with Stephen King becoming the first Cavanman to lift The Anglo-Celt Cup, following that 1997 Ulster final victory. The promise was not built on and stakeholders seemed to grow more impatient by the year, setting unrealistic goals.

As far back as the late 1970s, leading football historian Fr Dan Gallogly, in his book, *Cavan's Football Story*, would highlight emigration as a cause of the county's decline but also, depressingly, a "failure to admit there was a decline".

Cavan clung to the past, to a time when they were masters, and tended to believe they were still the kings of Ulster, just taking a break from the throne. A pattern set in. New manager, new team, promising start, defeat; new manager, new team... repeat to fade.

For a long time, Cavan supporters have commonly bemoaned the lack of an out-and-out scoring forward. Gene Cusack was an awesome scorer and the heir apparent to Gallagher but emigration to the United States stalled his progress and although a few individuals have emerged in the decades since and hinted at greatness, there has never been another Charlie.

In the years since he stopped playing, his memory has, naturally, faded. Had he won an All-Ireland medal or two, Gallagher — given how prolific he was, his longevity, his charisma — would undoubtedly be in the conversation when it came to the best inside forwards in history, from anywhere.

That he didn't was unfortunate but should not lessen the memory of the impact he made.

As it is, Charlie's name is still usually recalled in polls and lists of past greats and in conversations among old players and supporters who were there, who saw the word made flesh. Each year, though, their numbers dwindle.

In September, 2005, he was chosen by the listeners of Shannonside/Northern Sound radio as the greatest-ever footballer in their catchment area, which covers Cavan, Monaghan, Roscommon, Longford and Leitrim. Maureen collected the award at the event, which was broadcast live, remarking that Charlie "would have been in his element to think that he was worthy of such an award".

In 2011, the *Independent* printed, over the course of a few editions, a list of the greatest 125 footballers in Gaelic football history, chosen by a panel of experts. Gallagher was selected at 94; Kelly (122) and Carolan (119) were also included.

Three years later, he was an automatic choice at

full-forward on the best Cavan team of the last 50 years, as selected by the same newspaper.

For old colleagues and opponents, Charlie lives on. The Cavan team of that era remain quite close, a core group regularly meeting to play golf and shoot the breeze.

While they are happy with their lot in life, most agree that they should have lifted Sam. A common note they sound is that while Gallagher didn't always hit the high notes in Croke Park, there was a sense that the team was too dependent on him to do so.

"Until [Steve] Duggan or [Micheál] Greenan arrived, Charlie would say: 'Sure, I never had anyone to pass the ball to!'" Tom Lynch laughs.

"If we had one more quality forward, we would have won one or two All-Irelands. If Charlie had an off-day, we would struggle for scores, even if we were cleaning them out and winning possession.

"That's where we were beaten, we just fell short. Down had quality forwards and they played to a system. We were a bit naive now. It was okay to a point but to get the whole way, we were just that little bit off.

"It's easy to close down one player. But he was exceptional," says Lynch.

Frankie Kennedy agrees.

"If we had Genie Cusack along with Charlie earlier in the sixties, I think we'd have won two All-Irelands. You needed someone like him when you got to Croke Park. Charlie was brilliant in Ulster, he was unbeatable. But we needed a little bit more."

For Carolan, '67 was the one that got away. Others agree. Of all the Cavan teams that should have and could have, that was the one.

"Ah, we should have won an All-Ireland... There was no little bit of sitting down and saying 'this is what we have, this is what we need to do'.

"Down put more effort into it. I think they brought a new sense of preparation. But I would still say we were better than them. Without hesitation. We could beat them when we wanted to beat them. No fear, no nothing, we'd take them on.

"We could beat any team and we beat every team that won All-Irelands. We knew we were as good as any team and had no fear of any team. [But] there was obviously something missing.

"But we had ten good players and we were probably always short two or three."

Carolan's midfield partner for the guts of the decade was Lynch and before the ball was thrown in, Ray would sometimes remind Tom that they were the best pairing in the country. But luck went against them as much as anything.

"Our team in the sixties would remind you a bit of the Mayo team of the last few years," says Tom. "We were well capable of winning it but lacked a bit of firepower up front at times, and out of luck a bit, too. With a hop of the ball, one way or another, we could have won a couple of All-Irelands."

Back in the 1960s, it seemed the world was still young and for Cavan footballers, anything was still possible. But something died that wet day in Croke Park. It, too, washed away with those dressing room tears, spilled deep in the bowels of the stand.

The team broke up. The following decade was the first in which Cavan failed to win an Ulster title, losing two finals. They lost another in 1983 to Donegal, when Gabriel Kelly was in charge, and went a dozen years before making the big day again, losing heavily to Tyrone.

The 1997 success saw an eruption of joy in the county; almost three decades of frustration spilling out, but it, too, dissipated. There has been some recent success at underage level and in league football but at the time of writing, despite reaching a first Ulster final in 18 years in the summer of 2019, the wait for major success goes on.

Nobody knew it — or maybe, somewhere deep down, they did — but the close of 1969 marked the end of an era, of Charlie in the blue of Cavan and the end, once and for all, of Cavan as a powerhouse of the game.

Seamus Hoare, Railway Cup teammate and Ulster Championship foe, sums it up. "Charlie," he says, "was a bright light in the dark. A man like him comes along every 50 years."

That half-century has now passed. The hordes of Breffni faithful live in hope.

¶ ¶ ¶ ¶

Maureen Gallagher resides in Cootehill, where she is a popular member of the community, and her home is a warm and friendly place and surprisingly free of football memorabilia. There are bits and pieces here and there — jerseys and photos but no medals of substance. Charlie put no value on them.

Around the corner are her daughter Louise and son Peter. Adrian, the eldest, lives in Carrickfergus, Co Antrim. The family are close and greatly respected.

Sometimes, they will, by chance, meet someone of a

certain vintage, get to chatting as Irish people do and see that familiar glint in the eye as connection is made and the realisation dawns that they are speaking to Charlie Gallagher's offspring. There remains a great swathe of people, children of a particular time, who adore the man. They smile when that happens.

The Gallagher children were not steeped in the game growing up — it would have been impossible to follow in their father's footsteps. Their father didn't go on about his achievements although, once, Charlie did bring Adrian and Peter to Croke Park, the old stage he had graced so often, on a random weekday for a look around. Little did they realise the relevance of it all.

"Growing up, football was never a part of our lives. It really wasn't. I often wondered was that purposeful on his behalf," says Peter.

After Charlie died, they came to realise what an icon he had been but to them, he was Dad, nothing more or less.

All of Charlie's grandchildren cherish the memory of the grandad they never met. When Peter's daughter Ellen was given a project at school — tasked with writing a letter to a person she had never met — she chose her grandfather.

And Peter's son bears his name. They say he's showing great potential.

¶ ¶ ¶ ¶

Brian Gallagher died in 2008. His obituary remarked on how uncommonly decent he was, how he put no stock on money or material possessions. He was a beloved figure in Cootehill and elsewhere.

It was a trait he shared with his brother. When he worked in his home town, Charlie charged very little if anything. Often, patients from farming backgrounds would drop him in eggs or the odd pheasant as payment. Charlie was happy to accept.

In 2014, the building on Market Street where the Gallagher family were reared, where Brian and his father before him practised medicine and where Charlie set up a dentistry practice on his return from Derry, was officially handed over to Drumlin House — a wonderful organisation which provides opportunities for young people with intellectual disabilities.

There has been no monument erected to the memory of Charlie Gallagher, as MJ Clarke says, barring his headstone. Charlie is buried at St Michael's graveyard. Around him are his parents, his brothers, Brian and Fr Frank, and some of the finest footballers ever to wear the famous green and white of Cootehill Celtic. A local man, a football man, tends to these graves.

¶ ¶ ¶ ¶

Song and story. When people are brushed by magic, they don't forget it. If you were there when Charlie stuck the ball in the net and gave a wink to the crowd, or when he threw a jersey to a kid or strutted into a ball-room, styled and vital, you will remember it.

More than anything, what lingers is the warmth. Charlie's family have the fondest memories of their husband and father. His other family, his teammates, are the same.

"It's only when you look back that you see," says Tom Lynch.

"He was a famous footballer but the best thing about Charlie Gallagher, to me, was the man he was, his personality. He was the nicest fella you ever met. There wasn't a bad bone or thought in his body. He was just for fun. He was a lad who never grew up, like an under-fourteen being one of the top sportsmen in Ireland. He was one in a million."

The writer Shane Connaughton remembers Gallagher bestriding the stage in Killyfana, outside Redhills, a patch of grass on the side of a hill in the late 1950s.

"When Drung came to play, they arrived on bicycles. Cootehill came by car. Charlie Gallagher was always the first one we looked out for. We kids stood a few yards away from him, admiring him, thrilled, afraid because he and Cootehill in those days were almost unbeatable," says Connaughton.

"Always smiling, he wasn't an aloof figure. The game was his toy. Once only we saw him robbed. On a solo run towards goal, ready to shoot, our local hero, Max McGrath, nipped in and stole the ball from him. The crescendo of cheering was not only for Max. It was proof positive that Charlie Gallagher was the greatest footballer we ever saw."

Greatness is impossible to define but we know the one that has it. He was a splash of colour in a sepia-tinted photograph. A point from the corner flag. A gleaming, generous smile. A brilliant one-liner to warm a cold dressing room, as steel-toe boots rattle on the concrete.

In traditional drama, the tragic-hero is superhuman in all but one characteristic — which proves fatal. Charlie was that. The laughing boy of Cootehill, the lovable, generous adult adored by thousands, the magnificent sportsman, the star.

But stars burn out and this one, all too soon.

"He had the looks, the strength, the majesty," says Connaughton.

"The game seemed easy to him. It's life we find difficult."

Charlie Gallagher
Roll Of Honour

- Ulster Senior Football Championship 1962, 1964, 1967 (captain), 1969 (captain)
- Railway Cup 1964, 1965, 1966, 1968 (captain)
- Cavan Senior Football Championship 1954, 1955
- Cavan Intermediate Football Championship 1971
- Cavan Junior Football Championship 1969
- Cavan Senior League 1955, 1972
- Cavan Intermediate Football League 1971
- Dublin Senior League 1958
- MacRory Cup 1955
- Sigerson Cup 1959-60
- Wembley Tournament 1966, 1967 (captain)
- John F Kennedy Memorial Games 1964
- Cuchulainn Award 1964
- Cavan Team of the Millennium — right corner-forward
- Irish Nationwide *Sunday Independent* Team of the Century Never To Have Won an All-Ireland — left corner-forward
- Top scorer in Ireland 1964 (6-107), 1965 (7-102)
- Highest scorer in Cavan senior football history (49-674 in 190 matches).

Index

About The Author

Paul Fitzpatrick is the Sports Editor
of *The Anglo-Celt* newspaper in Cavan.

He was recognised for the quality of his work
after winning the Local Ireland Sports
Story of the Year award this year.

Paul previously wrote the acclaimed book
*The Fairytale In New York:
The Story of Cavan's Finest Hour.*

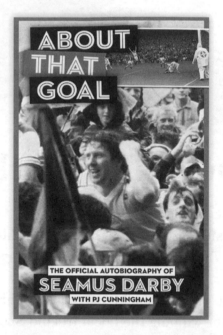

About That Goal
The Official Autobiography
of Seamus Darby
With PJ Cunningham

Inside this official autobiography, former Offaly star Seamus Darby talks about the sense of destiny he felt in the run-up to scoring arguably the most famous goal in the history of Gaelic football.

Darby also puts the record straight on rumours that have followed him around almost since that dramatic All-Ireland winning day against Kerry in 1982.

Visit www.ballpointpress.ie for more details.